THE MISSING LINK

BUILDING QUALITY TIME WITH TEENS

Stephen Allen
SHECHTMAN
&
Mark J.
SINGER

ABINGDON PRESS
NASHVILLE

THE MISSING LINK: BUILDING QUALITY TIME WITH TEENS

Library of Congress Cataloging in Publication Data

SHECHTMAN, STEPHEN, 1951–
The missing link.
Bibliography: p. Includes index.
1. Youth—Family relationships.
2. Parent and child. 3. Adolescence.
I. Singer, Mark, 1941– . II. Title.

HQ796.S4427 1985 646.7′8 85-9039

ISBN 0-687-27078-2

The table from *Developmental Tasks and Education,* Third Edition, by Robert J. Havighurst, is Copyright © 1972 by Longman Inc., reprinted by permission of Longman Inc., New York.

Portions of some chapters appeared originally in the following columns in the Accent on Living section of *The Globe-Times,* Bethlehem, Pennsylvania: "What Is TV Teaching Your Kids?" (February 12, 1984); "Whatever Happened to Innocence of Chidhood?" (May 20, 1984); "With School Out, M-TV Has Even Less Competition" (July 15, 1984); "IQ Is Only Part of the Story" (August 19, 1984).

MANUFACTURED BY TH PARTHENON PRESS AT
NASHVILLE, TENNESSEE, UNITED STATES OF AMERICA

To

Our mothers and fathers, who helped us realize the importance of parent/teen relationships and their ultimate effect on our development

Our children, David, Becky, and Seth, who, although not yet teenagers, will help us continue to experience the challenge of parenting

Sandra J. Donald, who taught us about reconciliation, making this collaborative effort possible

and to

Jane O'Donnell, who, through her constructive criticism, key editorial comments, and frequent moral support, was instrumental in the completion of this task—

We dedicate this book to all of you.

And finally, we would like to thank the members of the Virginia Commonwealth University secretarial staff, who were able to revise portions of this manuscript on such short notice. Our thanks go especially to Kim Hughes.

CONTENTS

PREFACE

Raising a teen today is a tremendously complicated task. On one hand, parents must unscramble the changes they are undergoing as they enter mid-life, while at the same time attempting to relate to adolescents who demand their own right to do as they please. On the other hand, the world in which we raise children is vastly different from the one in which we were raised. So parents of teens must adjust their internal picture of the ideal family, juggling their own needs with their teens' needs. This book focuses on the nature of parent and teen changes and highlights the building of meaningful relationships between teens and parents, in spite of the demands and fast pace of our society.

As you become familiar with the ideas addressed in this book, you will note that the sequence of content is important. We begin with an overall discussion of quality time, along with some special items concerning the parent/teen relationship. Chapter 2 contrasts adolescent and parent developmental issues, with emphasis on the interaction between adolescent development and the numerous parental life-crisis issues. Chapter 3 focuses on family stresses and describes four types of family behavior, which break down into sixteen categories. Chapter 4 elaborates on parent/teen interaction with the "at-risk" issues present during the adolescent's development. In Chapter 5, some of the earlier content is applied, with comments on ways to actually build better relationships between parents and teenagers. And finally, as a method of assessing relationships, Chapter 6 provides a number of evaluative measures, so that both teens and parents may examine the present tone of their interaction and decide on the direction they wish to take. (The authors suggest that both teen and parent complete the first three family forms in Chapter 6 before reading beyond this Preface.) Resources for parents and teens are listed in the back of the book.

The traditional family of the working father and housewife mother has been outnumbered by two-salaried and single-parent families. Today's society gives teens more power, freedom, and distance from parent figures, and these changes create a different focus of attention between teen and parent. In order to understand the way you interact with your teen, it is necessary to look at the history of the relationship. You might ask, "How did I, as a parent, get along with my child during the childhood years?" The clues to your present interaction with your teen may be found in pieces of family background, or it may be more of a problem now as you deal with mid-life issues. You might ask if the times you spent together earlier were abbreviated or were not altogether casual or relaxed. Members of a two-career family often spend time with one another during the dinner hour, but not a great deal more because of the nature of their individual interests or perhaps the pressures of work brought home from the office. Single-parent families have other stresses that diminish quality time. Quality time is complicated even more by the fact that teens leave their families and pursue their own interests in the midst of an environment filled with the recreational use of drugs, open sexual mores, and economic and technological changes. Parents must adjust to the fact that many teens want to be out with friends or involved in activities apart from their parents or siblings.

The journey from childhood to adolescence and from adolescence to young adulthood has been described in many ways—from conflictual or chaotic to conservative or conforming. Developmentally, adolescence can prove to be a long, strained period for both parent and teen. While the teen struggles with a series of life issues, the parent may be experiencing either a resurgence of earlier life concerns, or a conflict with present career and identity. This dynamic between teen and parent can affect the quality of interaction. In fact, there appears to be a frequent parting of the ways and, in essence, an early breakdown of communication between teen and adult which limits personal and family growth.

In addition to the many changes of adolescence and

the life-stage issues facing parents within the context of a complex world, there are different family types—from those that are open and supportive to those that are adversarial, self-defeating, and either over- or underinvolved in their reactions. Many parents and teens negatively cue each other so as to become self-defeating in their interaction. The teen may feel forced to go his or her own way. Or, if parent and teen each respect the newly formed independence and ability of the other, they may achieve an interdependent and cooperative relationship. Teens and parents *can* bridge and maintain channels of communication within the push and pull of individual wills. The task is not to establish adversarial roles, but rather to develop quality relationships.

This book can help you examine the type of relationship you currently have in your family, and the type you want. It can help you build quality moments together. We hope that some of the ideas spark a sense of creative optimism as teens and parents make attempts to understand the others' world. Quality relationships between family members require reflective thought and honest communication. Quality time develops as members work together to find positive solutions to situations that frequently appear unsolvable. The first key step: *Note what you say and do.* Second: *assess* its positive and/or negative effect. And third: *limit negative while multiplying positive* interaction.

THE MISSING LINK

CHAPTER 1

Quality Time: The Essential Ingredient

So you want a quality relationship with your teenager. But are you really willing to become more aware of what you do and say? Are both you and your teen ready to evaluate the history and nature of your interaction? Quality time and a quality relationship are compatible notions, not elusive conditions—even during the adolescent years! However, the demands of modern life often tend to detract from the amount of quality time parent and teen give each other. Family members are overloaded by expectations from a variety of sources. Career, school, and self-related issues determine the amount of time spent with one another and the nature of the time spent. If we become locked into those scheduled activities we see as necessities, then we become slaves to the routines and fail to talk and do things together. It is the routine events—the car pooling, the meetings after school or work, and the countless other responsibilities that bear upon us—that sometimes detract from our enjoyment of one another.

Interestingly, as discussed later, these very routine activities can be utilized creatively to bring about moments of quality time.

How can an enriched relationship between parent and adolescent be created? A first step is to examine the way family members interact with one another. For example, there are four general types of interaction which essentially describe most family patterns. The members of *cooperative* families relate to one another openly, discuss differences without fear of criticism, and are generous with affection. These families demonstrate growth-oriented behavior while coping effectively with teen and adult developmental concerns. If a teen is experiencing a problem with a particular area of development—for example, facial or bodily appearance—family members are sensitive to one another's needs and do not ignore the teen's concern in this area.

The *adversarial* family is composed of individuals who work against one another when handling either crises or routine events of the day. These people are unable to talk freely about subjects that cause concern; they send double messages to one another (sometimes unknowingly) and are frequently unaware of their real feelings. For these families, routine situations become crises and take on an unnecessary sense of negativism and gloom. These crises become predictable and tend to isolate family members from one another. An example might involve a teenage girl who has recently experienced her first sexual relationship with her new boyfriend. In this particular situation the experience proved unrewarding, and the girl would like to tell her mother. However, she senses that she will receive a great deal of criticism, because in this family, "good" girls don't become sexually involved. Instead of an open line of communication between parent and teen, there is a door kept closed to meaningful dialogue. Family members are quick to judge and criticize one another before hearing what the others have to say.

We have observed that overly critical or adversarial parents can create an environment where teens frequently act in opposition to their parents, even when it is against their own best interests. In cases where behaviors demonstrate errors of judgment, reactions of family members need not be critical. To admit a mistake and say "I'm sorry" shows compassion and allows individuals to demonstrate a sense of humanness. Some families have difficulty doing even this.

The *overinvolved* family members appear very supportive on the surface, but become overly connected or attached to other family members and their concerns. In this situation, we might see a parent who is generally functioning on an effective level with a teenager struggling with normal adolescent adjustments or one who is experiencing more serious medical problems. The parent begins by acting as an "essential support person" but becomes so involved that neither the teen nor the parent experiences a sense of growth. Although this family intends its outlook on life to be meaningful, the members' actions have a stifling effect.

Finally, in the fourth family type, the members are detached, or *underinvolved* in the life of the family. In a family in which the parents have remarried, one or both may not be emotionally ready to meet family demands and may detach themselves from much of the family's time together.

Both the third and fourth family units described here often seem slightly out of balance, though certain family members may pick up the loose ends that go unattended.

These family categories generally represent the types of situations we find as part of family life. In order to evaluate and perhaps eliminate problems in your family, the task for both teen and parent is to decide where their family fits in relation to these categories. This can be done by looking at the figure titled "A Family Typology." Try to visualize yourself on one of the two axes which represent the family types that have been described.

A FAMILY TYPOLOGY

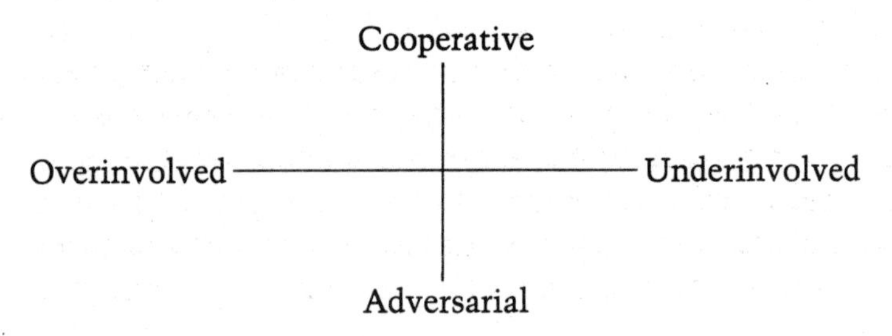

Once you have done this, you have begun to move toward a greater degree of self-awareness. Later, in Chapter 3, these four typologies will be expanded to illustrate sixteen categories, which allows for a more in-depth assessment of parent/teen relationships.

Quality time should be seen as *unhurried, uncritical,* and *undivided.* Although these are not new concepts, time spent in this fashion has positive significant meaning. We believe that to enhance quality time, we must look at the needs of parents and teens and at the strengths of each. Quality time that is unhurried, uncritical, and undivided allows adults and teens the opportunity to attach positive value to both routine and special events in which they take part. These times together serve as building blocks which establish a sense of trust, rapport, and open communication between young people and their parents.

Given the pace of the world in which we live, bringing about an unhurried existence with one another is essential. Being unhurried implies that we want to be with the other person in a relaxed manner, with time not a major factor. Second, parent and teen can then identify with, focus upon each other, and feel united. They can attend to each other rather than complain about school, other kids, business, or other self-oriented concerns. Finally, relationships that are accepting and compassionate give both teen and parent a sense of trust and positive regard. Within a noncritical atmosphere people can feel accepted and risk making mistakes without fear of judgment.

Generally, all parents will experience conflict with their teen as they attempt to influence their child's overall development. Many teens will view their parents' involvement as conflictual, at worst, or meddling, at best, as they search for a separate identity. How this period is reconciled will determine the quality of the relationship.

When we consider the earlier discussion of life stresses, it seems important to integrate these basic concepts into the idea of quality time. Teens and parents do have their own separate worlds, worlds that are quite hurried and fast-paced. During the interplay between these apparently separate life spheres, teens are striving for their own sense of autonomy and identity, while parents frequently seem to overstep these emotional boundaries.

Additionally, parents are struggling with their own life crises—crises which concern significant self-issues; this focus often contributes to a split between teen and parent, since undivided attention to the teen is not always possible because of the emotional place in which adults seem to find themselves. Further, parents' concern about self-issues often results in the projection of their thoughts, desires, images, and fears onto the teen. This may bring about two conditions. The first involves an intrusion of the parent into the life of the teen—the parent may become overly protective and cautious. This situation gives the adolescent little room to experience new environments for growth. A second condition may develop—the parent may become highly critical or place unrealistic expectations upon the teen; these situations either diminish the teen's self-image or push the teen into activities that may prove jeopardizing.

Special Components

When we speak of quality time between teens and parents, we begin to realize the unique nature of the relationship that is developing. Adolescence is a transition time with periods of cyclical behavior for both teens and adults. As we elaborate on these changes, it becomes evident that quality family time between parents and teens requires a sensitivity on both their parts to these changing patterns of behavior. Therefore, in further defining quality efforts, we note a variety of conditions that will need nurturing if positive relationships are to be developed.

A Caring Attitude. Frequently, a teen's world is filled with experiences that are "horribly painful" to share, especially with a parent. Eliciting information about a particular incident does not mean that the parent smothers the teen with concern. Instead, a more patient attitude should be demonstrated by a great deal of listening. For example, it is especially helpful to know how to talk with a teen about an experience—the loss of a girlfriend or boyfriend—without casting judgment.

Respect for Subjective Views. This is a tough one for many parents and adolescents—it reflects the ability of each to at least hear the other point of view. Teens have developed the cognitive ability to evaluate the world in a way that is similar to their parents'. However, their views are often myopic and self-centered. Teens possess a tremendous amount of idealism which usually contains opinions that are refreshing and worthy of hearing. The difficulty here is that teens will frequently refute, disagree, and turn off any ideas suggested by parents. The "no adult knows" attitude held by adolescents is a real deterrent to a relationship with open communication and positive regard.

Likewise, some parents act much the same when they refuse to at least hear and give credence to the beliefs, values, and opinions of their teenagers. They say, "What do you know, you've never worked!" or "You haven't lived long enough to know how to get along in this world." This type of criticism does a great deal to impair effective relationships, since it shuts down communication.

Belief in the Complex Nature of Adolescence. We have often heard a parent tell a teen, "If you think you have it tough now, you should have seen what I went through when *I* was your age." Or again, "I had trouble growing up when I was a teenager—no reason why you shouldn't." These sorts of comments discount individual differences and create distance by isolating the teenager. Theygeneralize, making the teen feel lacking in any unique reactions that are a part of an emerging identity. The teen years are problematic for many youths and need not be viewed as overly simplistic, but in the same vein, they do not necessitate an overreaction on the parent's part. A degree of empathy is called for, and parents can achieve this concern by remembering their own teen years.

Being Separate But Close. It is essential that both the teen and the parent be allowed some space and a degree of autonomy. Adolescents desperately need to believe that they are persons in their own right, that they have significance in their home and community. Teens need to make their own decisions, even those that may go against their best interests. The teen who asks his or her parents for the car after committing a traffic violation needs to be allowed renewed responsibility to drive. Similarly, the parents who see their teen entering a relationship where he or she may be emotionally hurt might consider allowing that space and monitoring the teen's reaction to this love relationship. These consequences are hard sometimes, but need to be experienced, especially if there is parental support available "after the fall"! In these cases an adult serves the relationship best not by preaching, but rather by allowing the teen to make individual choices.

Interestingly, there are payoffs for parents who allow such space. Giving the teen an opportunity to grow and make some independent decisions frees the adult from becoming overly distressed about "what might happen." When adults allow teens more autonomy, they establish a situation of trust.

Additionally, as teens assume more responsibility, parents experience lessened anxiety and concern. Such a situation contributes to a workable relationship between adolescents and parents. It allows parents an opportunity to pursue their own self-interests while giving teens the autonomy toward which they strive.

Open Expression of Feelings. Parents and teens need to demonstrate caring and empathy. Expressing feelings about issues in a noncritical manner will allow both parties the opportunity to, in turn, elicit feelings at critical points. Often we need to place ourselves in the shoes of the other person. How do things appear from the other's perspective? For example, if a teen comes home from school having had a major conflict with a teacher, don't be too quick to judge the child or the teacher. There are two sides to every story. The ability to listen or probe without intrusion or judgment is the key to persuading the teen to share feelings more frequently.

In like fashion, the adult who comes home from work also may need time to vent emotions and have someone listen before being willing to consider the needs of others. Take time with each other so as to appreciate the other's world.

Factors Working Against Quality Time

The comments above seem all well and good, yet parents and teens sometimes work against one another, inhibiting quality moments. As adults, our reactions to the period of adolescence is to lament, "Will it ever end?" If this message is communicated to the teen by word or action, it tends to block the founding of quality adult/teen relationships. In other words, parents can set up an adversarial role when this type of pessimistic signal is sent. It is better to view adolescence as a time of important developmental change. The way the teen deals with this change determines the degree of "crisis" experienced. There will seemingly be both progress and regression in behavior and attitudes. Setbacks in establishing quality time arise when adults become nonchalant toward the creation of an environment of caring and trust. Typically, the "will it ever end" attitude leads to other relationship-defeating characteristics.

Parents become angry when teens do not meet their expectations or follow some sort of direction. Teens tend to be contrary in their attitudes and will respond negatively if pushed too hard. They can be oppositional and will "cut off their noses to spite their faces." On the other hand, some parents relive their own adolescence, remembering when they struggled with their own unresolved needs. Whether it be relationships the teen is forming with others outside the home or a defiance of authority which reminds many parents of their own past conflicts, the adult becomes seduced into identifying with particular adolescent issues or concerns. If parents over-identify with these issues, they can be seen as overly involved, a situation that sets up conditions for a power/control-problem relationship.

Testing of limits is an agony that goes on perpetually between teen and parent, causing frustration that acts as a block to the reduction of conflict or stress. Parents experience weariness as teens continually test limits in an attempt to develop their own identity. The point here remains that testing is to be expected and, within bounds, can be allowed. Teens need space to grow and nurture new skills. In fact, we know that, developmentally, during the period of middle adolescence (from 15–18), teens strive for and need to achieve a greater amount of independence and control over their own lives. As parents, we must try to give them this room.

Parents become defensive when teens discount adult values and life-styles, believing that only they can see the world as it really is. Some youths view their parents as materialistic, with a perspective of the world that is quite limited, or, at best, as inflexible in their values. (By the way, parents believe the same about teens.) Rather than becoming defensive, parents could try to be more curious or open about the ideas teens hold. Some conversations can be tense if they confront adult values. Expect that adults are going to be challenged—cognitively and emotionally—for this is where the teen is. If parents can utilize this challenge by turning it into some type of creative plateau or dialogue, then an adversarial situation can be altered to one with more learning and growth potential. By reducing the necessity to continually defend, parents can spend more energy on the interests and tasks that surround their own lives.

Being *insensitive to teens' evaluation of themselves* can cause further difficulty. As parents, we make errors of omission as well as commission. We often forget the bench marks teens use in evaluating their total performance against those of others their age. At times it is extremely difficult for adults to understand the world of teenagers and relate to the kinds of issues they face—everything from clothing and physical appearance to drug use can be a basis for comparison. Being cued into the behaviors, thoughts, and feelings of the teen helps the parent comprehend the way the teen perceives his or her self-image—a critical variable in development.

Finally, *adults are often confused* about when they should engage the adolescent and when they can separate themselves from the parent role. It is a fine line that parents walk, and often they become either overly involved or quite disengaged, distant. Parents and teens have difficulty finding a happy medium as to the amount of control or involvement they should have with one another. The needs of the family and of the individuals in the family warrant consideration here. The confusion is lessened when we realize that an environment in which people have opportunities for self-expression is the most valuable asset the family can build. There needs to be an open flow of ideas, where people share their lives.

CHAPTER 2

Clashing Worlds: Adolescent and Adult Development

Books, magazines, and countless television specials have focused upon the adolescent years and the traumas connected wih that period. The crises experienced within the middle-adult phase of living have also been given special emphasis. However, it is not often that we view these two worlds together and consider the effects they have upon each other. These parallel life-stage developments often add to the complexity of effective relationships between parents and child.

For example, adolescence is characteristically a time when youths confront a series of developmental issues—relationships with friends, school performance, career readiness, sexual identity, and questions about physical and emotional intimacy. It is a period filled with attachments to fads, idols, close friends, and high ideals, a passing from the sometimes comfortable womb of childhood to the mercurial years of "teenhood."

It would be one thing if the basic question were only the passage of adolescent development, but this frequently is complicated by the natural and normal life crisis of the mid-adult years, a period much like adolescence, filled with change and self-doubt. It is a time when adults begin a process of self-reflection regarding a number of critical areas—careers, the quality of life, financial stability, changing relationships with spouse, adjustment to aging parents. They also are realizing some of the potential physical changes that will eventually take place and maintaining a network of associations in the broader community, not to mention the sometimes difficult task of watching teens grapple with the conditions of adolescent growth. As these life concerns become entangled with those of the teen, major trouble spots can emerge and detract from positive or meaningful family relationships. However, consistent and coherent adjustment by either teen or adult can minimize the degree of conflict and eventual confrontation.

We need to look at the changes adults and teenagers are separately undergoing, and at how these changes affect their two worlds simultaneously. We also need to note how these worlds come into conflict and the way family members can find some positive interchange. Reflectively, adolescence is like a brave new country which the teen shifts through on the journey from childhood. Parents and teen find living together difficult, since they often work against each others' needs. The teen is striving to become a separate person, while parents are reëxamining the conditions of their own lives.

Key Issues in Adolescence

An initial review of the adolescent transition helps set a base line for our thinking about relationships between teens and adults. Although many parents believe they understand the evolving concerns of their teenager, the real significance of this period may go unattended by many. Adolescence, like adulthood, is a time of crises—not necessarily in the negative sense. The Greeks defined crisis as dividing and growing: New experiences of life allow us an opportunity to build our sense of self. And so it is with the adolescent/parent situation.

For many teens and parents, developmental crises do not bring about comfortable times. Although some families are well prepared and adaptable, others find this period as agonizing as a bad toothache. Understanding the changes that are going on for both teen and parent is the first step, but finding a way to negotiate those changes is another matter.

Adolescence: A Leap for Life

For most, the immediate difference in the movement from childhood is the physical explosion that occurs because of bodily change. These changes are frequently significant as they project a youth quickly into an adult world. One might ponder the fact that barely one hundred years ago, a young boy might have helped load the Conestoga wagon and headed West to strike out on his own. Our society has changed. In part, our technological age has forced us to lengthen the period of adolescence. Too, the increased life span may have extended the period of preparation for adulthood so that teens spend more time in the home before they are grown.

Parents attempt to project their values and control over children who are striving to act autonomously. For example, many parents do not condone premarital sexual behavior for teens, yet some teens place heavy emphasis on sexual experimentation. Teens face decisions concerning intimate relationships well before they leave their parents' home. An adolescent boy may tell his mother he is going to a friend's house, but end up sleeping in his girlfriend's backyard. Or a fourteen-year-old young woman may have been car-dating since she was twelve, yet withholding this information, as best she can, from her parents.

Specific Changes

Physiologically, teens are preoccupied with several bodily changes, which occur at varying rates in each person. Everything from facial and body hair to breast and genital size brings on concern and questions: What will I do with my hair? How do I cover up these pimples? And the ultimate question—How do I measure up and compare? There is status in being the first to develop breasts or facial hair. In contrast, the late bloomer can feel inadequate and embarrassed. All are serious passage questions for the adolescent.

Emotionally, some teens may be like firecrackers, ready to blow up at the first spark of conflict. Others react with a longer fuse that minimizes explosions. Adults need to remember that emotional changes naturally accompany the biochemical alterations that are taking place. Emotions are cyclical for some and rather tempered for others. One minute teens can feel they are floating on a cloud, while later it's as if they were sinking in an ocean of despair. In the early stages of adolescence, usually between thirteen and fifteen, these swings are even more severe. Some teens describe this early period as "pure panic." Their search for an emerging identity can be overwhelming. Teens feel the stress to own different clothing styles, try new behaviors and mannerisms—their teen life is a series of changing roles. Generally the emotional roller coaster evens off during later adolescence, around sixteen to eighteen, when identity issues begin to firm up.

Cognitive changes are also taking place. Teens are now able to think abstractly and conceptualize the world. Rational and logical thinking begins to develop, and teens are better able to verbally confront the adults around them.

Essentially, personality and bodily changes are the bottom line from which other areas of the teen's world evolves. These changes, along with the world in which the adolescent lives, demand special understanding and sensitivity from the parent—an understanding not steeped in overprotectiveness, intrusion, or control, but a healthy balance of support and guidance, with occasional limit setting. Parents should be frank and open about the changes that either will or have already begun to take place. The amount of directness and openness will depend partially upon the nature of the parent/teen relationship prior to adolescence. That relationship could even be enhanced if, during preadolescence, parents could initiate talks about the normal transitions that will occur. This preparation can provide useful information that could alleviate a certain amount of frustration and anxiety for everyone.

Everybody Tune In!

It is particularly critical that teen and adult understand each other's needs if quality relationships are to develop. It is the symbolic and active everyday world in which both live that is important. This world varies from family to family, but most contain the essential elements. Attending to the basic needs of both adult and teen will bridge gaps and build, or possibly rebuild, relationships.

For the teen, emotional, physical, and cognitive changes are the basic ingredients for this period's growth. As noted earlier, these are the crisis points that actually mark the transition from childhood by moving the adolescent onto a higher level of functioning. Parents occasionally take these changes for granted or are insensitive to their impact.

As a parent, your awareness not only of what is

happening, but of your teen's unique response to this upheaval is crucial. Remembering your own adolescent problems will help create empathy within you. Realizing, too, that there is a degree of myopia or self-centeredness which acts as a force on adolescents, isolating them from you and from the community, is a useful bit of knowledge. Conditions such as menstruation, body physique, and just plain old acne can make life miserable for the teenager.

What changes does the adult undergo? For the adult, there may be a similar question regarding physical or emotional variances. We are a body-conscious, health-oriented society. Both men and women work very hard to keep fit. Those of us who take time to keep in shape can become quite zealous about our physical well-being. Parents of teens may also be experiencing emotional changes, some of which may have a physiological base while others may be due to a change in status, need for satisfaction of self, or a host of other concerns typical of the approach to mid-life. The point here is that although adults are not involved in new changes, they may be reexperiencing a resurgence of generalized change. Their focus may be slightly different, and their tolerance for the changes occurring in a teenage son or daughter may only create conflict. The sharing of concerns between parent and teen can alert both to the common issues they are facing. An overall understanding of these basic areas can begin to alleviate tension.

Peers and Friends

"I'm going out with Bob." "I'll be seeing Lisa tonight." These are refrains parents may hear if they are lucky! Parents worry a great deal about their teens' friends and associates. At times parents may not know clearly who those friends really are. There's a saying that you can choose your friends but not your relatives. Teens usually choose their friends wisely, but this is not always the case. Generally, adolescents need their peer group as a way to develop and work out their forming identities. Sometimes these alliances with friends will be short-lived—a week, a month—but at other times they are the basis for lifelong relationships. Parents should be sensitive to the importance of peer relationships to the teen, without letting themselves become entangled in the friendships or push too hard to persuade the teen to relate. Neither should they be too cautious of teen friendships or try to end those friendships. In other words, parents should remain parents. A mother—trying to look attractive to the boyfriend her daughter brings home—may style her hair, wear clothes more appropriate for her daughter, and actually compete for attention. Mom wants to look really "cool," but she goes to extremes. In such a case, the mother may have unresolved issues about her own identity. The point here is that parents need to be separate from, but interested in, the life of their teen; becoming overinvolved serves no useful function and can create jealous arguments.

Peers are critical for teenage growth. A close friend, a confidant, the girls, the gang, the immediacy of some form of sharing is paramount. The ups and downs of adolescence often rest on the nature of the teen's relationships with friends. For some teens, friends are the only stable feature in their lives, even though the emotional turmoil friendships can cause is extremely trying. Some peer relationships can prove detrimental. It is hard for parents to let their teen make choices. What if they're out joyriding and there's an accident? What if they're using drugs or alcohol? What about all the free sex! The list could go on endlessly, and there's no easy answer for these concerns. The best alternative is to monitor, not dictate, teen behavior. Granted the line is very thin, and you frequently find yourself biting your lip—very hard. Keep in mind that the more you attempt to control the teen and deny free choice, the more distance you create between yourself and your son or daughter. It is analogous to holding sand in your palm and squeezing very hard—it just slips through your fingers.

Peer Relationships During Middle Adulthood

For the parent, the issue of peer relationships and friendships also is complex. We see this on two levels. First, parents identify with the developmental conflicts of their teens and remember their struggles during their own adolescence. All the questions facing their teens are now being relived in the minds of the adults. Past concerns are reflected and determine how the parents respond to these issues now being confronted by their son or daughter. Assuredly, mothers and fathers have different perspectives in viewing their teens' growth—fathers' view of sons versus fathers' view of daughters is not the same as mothers' relationships with sons or daughters. As a parent, if you've come to grips with your own particular life-stage concerns and can be objective about how your son or daughter is handling his or her development, then your relationship with your teen can be much more productive. On another level, parents come in contact with other parents who also have teens. Comparisons are made regarding a teen's school performance, material possessions, clothes, and career aspirations, and parents begin to live their lives through the achievements of their teens. Adult relationships are important, but should focus more on adult leisure-time activities and topics of interest.

The World of Music

Music is the lifeline of most teens. Whether it be pop, jazz, rock, hard rock, country, soul, blues, or the classics, it serves as a clear focus for many youths. In one respect music is a way of tuning out the adult world, a way of escape into a type of fantasy life—a life that becomes a reality. Music—lyrics and notes—solidifies and gives meaning to a time when meanings are lost.

There may be levels of sophistication through which teens attach themselves to their music. Music today, as in years past, is tightly woven, with a variety of symbols, movements, and rhythms, and, most important, it contains a source of energy. It is a way of coming into contact with an exciting and glittering world of different people, clothes, behaviors, and wonderful stories teens share with one another. It helps supply a "role" for them to fit into.

Parents' most difficult task is to appreciate, or at least be sensitive toward this particular facet of the teen world. Some of the music may not suit many parents at this point in their life. And probably their parents reacted with alarm to their immersion in the music of their day. Music changes year by year, decade to decade, and the names of musical groups are not as important as the purpose of the music. It might be helpful for you as a parent to recognize a particular tune by a particular group—this is impressive and may earn you points with your teen. (You never know, you may like what you hear!)

All this aside, the basic point is that music provides youth with critical roots which become an important part of their life-style. For example, music provides the content of an identity separate from the "mold" perceived by the teen. Fans attach themselves not always to a group, but to the ideas the group is singing about. Certain groups become associated with a particular sound and type of music; at one time, a large population of youth became identified with a phenomenon called Beatle mania.

Music provides a common basis for relating to other teens, soothes anxiety, and is a great way to spend free time.

Since the world of music is closely associated with the peer culture to which your child relates, you could better understand both your teen and the peer group through their music. This requires only an interest in exposing yourself to an important aspect of the teen world. Study the lyrics of the songs. Do they contrast with the values you hold?

As adults, we also can claim a musical heritage. An awareness of our own past, how it affected us, and how we now relate to music as a leisure-time activity can assist in the relationship we want to develop with a teen.

Teen Idols

Idols are varied and come from a variety of life circumstances—sports, TV, movies, music. Yet our heroes are not always associated with the limelight. A younger teen can revere an older teenager who seems experienced and more emancipated. Knowing this aids us in understanding a teen's desperate need for a sense of autonomy. Teens grow quickly; being "on your own" is a desire of many young people who, in reality, frequently can handle their own lives.

As adults, we need to realize that teens look for pieces of their own identity through their dreams and fantasies about their idols. Everyone has images of who they are. Interestingly, adults have serious questions about their identity during the mid-life period. Although parents may seem secure, they are frequently reflective about the person they've become. This process is heightened when they see their teenagers struggling with essential developmental questions. Parents may move through a similar phase as they examine the events and conditions in their own lives, careers, personal relationships, images of their physical and emotional self. Teens and parents who are aware of this "search," or reexamination of identity, can better appreciate the struggle and the reaction they may have toward one another.

Close Friends, Dating, and Social Intimacies

Peer relationships are critical to the teen. Friends of the same gender become compatriots and intimates when there is a need to share private concerns. A girl's best friend becomes a true confidant, to whom the most closely guarded secrets are revealed. And the relationship between two young men can be essential throughout their adolescent development. In addition, peer groups are common for teens. Hanging out or going to social gatherings with the "gang" is quite natural. The advantages of a cache of associates is that it may later lead to closer types of social relationships.

To the teen, social relationships are crucial. "I'll die if he doesn't look at me," is a cry commonly heard by parents. Finding a friend for a socially intimate relationship is a normal developmental task, an endeavor at which many adolescents expend much energy. Making social contacts during this time is a double-edged sword: There is both a repulsion and an attraction to becoming involved in close physical relationships with the opposite gender. For teens, social relationships are complex and, in fact, reflect a sort of dating continuum. On one end, we see adolescents who are quite introverted and uncomfortable in making any type of social contact, while at the other extreme we note those who are overinvolved both emotionally and physically to the point of developing a rather promiscuous life-style. In the middle range are the many youths who are concerned about their social involvement, with periods of both anxiety and normal expectation with regard to the dating process itself. Dating in our society is a major hurdle for teens. When issues of sexual experimentation enter in, it becomes much more complex. Sexual experimentation is as natural as breathing for more than just a few youths. These are the realities of our times. In a scene from the movie *On Golden Pond,* Henry Fonda and his thirteen-year-old house guest are discussing girls. Fonda asks, "Well, what do you do with girls?" Incredulous, he hears, "Well, you suck face"—a response that takes the crotchety Fonda back a few steps. You can almost see the wheels of his mind turning—"What's this *kid* doing with girls anyway?" And that's the point. Sexual behaviors vary across the entire teen population. Effective parents react in a very nonjudgmental manner, showing understanding of the nature of peer involvement and pressure. (David Elkind, *All Grown Up and No Place to Go*, notes that 70 percent of the teenage population has had a sexual experience before the 18th birthday.) An awareness of your own values as a parent and the value struggles of your teenage son or daughter requires a good deal of discussion. The decision on where to take a stand depends on the parent's values. It is a question for each individual: Can you accept your child's sexual activity while being true to your own values?

Overall, parents would do best to become attentive and empathic listeners. Being tuned in to your teen's needs and desires is the first step; being aware of your own feelings about the socially intimate behavior of your teen is a second. Yet there is a third ingredient. Adults, during mid-life, may be experiencing their own struggles regarding intimacy, either with a spouse or, in the case of a single parent, with an outside dating relationship. For intact and blended-family parents, a renewal or reexamination of their emotional and physical relationships may be important during the middle years. For single parents, the understanding of their own sexuality and intimate relationships with others may be an ongoing concern during this time.

The teen's attempt to form social relationships does not involve the same developmental issues as the adult's attempt. Yet though there are different levels and perceptions of intimacy, the needs of both teens and parents have common features. The most basic feature is the need to understand one's own physical and emotional self in regard to someone with whom a meaningful relationship can be formed. When parents can separate their own intimacy needs from the developmental concerns of adolescents, then a mutual sensitivity and understanding can occur.

Self-Concerns

Adolescents can be, and usually are quite self-centered. Their interests frequently revolve around the kind of image they want to project to others. In early adolescence, a primary focus is on the immediate bodily and emotional changes taking place; in the later teen years, fitting into a peer group and being recognized for having some ability or special skill is most important. The core question, nonetheless, is teens' often nagging concern about who they are and who they think they want to become. A teen's confidence is often built like a sand castle—it seems to vanish in an instant. There is tremendous ambivalence, in that at one moment the teen can be quite independent, then suddenly will retreat into a dependent state, needing an adult to come to the rescue.

For the adult, self-issues are also of concern during the mid-life period. The task is not to become so entangled in normal teen development that you lose sight of where you are as an adult parent. Each of you has your own questions to resolve. By being aware of these areas, both teen and parent can better understand the reactions each might have toward the other during this time, and thereby bring about a more compatible relationship.

Carrying On in Spite of Everything

Because of the nature of both adolescence and the mid-adult period of life, much seems to be happening—and generally is. Family members need to be sensitive to one another's particular place in life. Despite crises, people can manage not only to coexist, but also to nurture a very positive atmosphere. Much of what has been discussed is routine in the lives of most people. It becomes problematic when family members impose on one another's personal space, rather than allowing each person the opportunity to come to grips with the issues requiring resolution. Teens and parents not only can carry out daily routines, but actually will begin to find that their lives can blend together instead of clashing. If we take into consideration the important factors of both teen and adult development, then we can discover more effective ways to manage family relationships so that they reflect a positive and expanding environment.

CHAPTER 3

Quality Time: A Problem for New Era Families

Quality time may not be attainable in the same way in all families , but the question is, How can *you* achieve more quality time in *your* family? Quickly we begin to realize that the changing nature of our society poses realistic concerns for many Americans. The intact family unit is not necessarily the most statistically dominant in many communities. In fact, given the increasing divorce rate and economic changes, families with altered structures have become quite evident and normal. These include separated or divorced units, single-parent families, blended or merged families, and dual-career families—a structure that frequently cuts across all the others. Many families, because of these altered arrangements, experience a great deal of strain, and this makes quality family time even more elusive. The structure of a family will inevitably impact the nature of its members' life together. Additionally, the stress that family members perceive will reflect the tone of their interaction, in both time and quality. How does the structure of your family affect the way each of you interacts?

Many individuals today must adjust to a number of family conditions. Meeting the needs of both teens and adults becomes more complicated, since conflicting needs must fit in with the nature of the family's structure. We know it is stressful to live in many family situations—being a part of a single-parent home, a remarried family, or a two-career situation only adds to the difficulty of developing a positive family atmosphere. These stresses are critical when considering the needs of both adults and teens.

We sometimes wonder if the intact family structure is fast becoming a ghost of yesterday. Certainly, the nuclear family still exists—it has not disappeared. However, there is stress in even such an apparently intact unit; the same difficulties that affect other family types apply also to the nuclear family. Questions regarding family communication, decision making, planning of finances, scheduling of time for activities, and many other related adult/teen interactions are in evidence.

Blended Families: A New Coming Together

Blended or merged families are bombarded with a variety of stress-related factors that might keep the members from growing closer. Because two family systems have come together, the immediate concern involves the already existing perceptions of family life that each person brings to this new unit.

Additionally, children can sabotage the merged family, since its development signals the death of their fantasy that the biological parents will remarry. Everyone enters such a family structure with a different family history—a history that makes up a value base regarding the understanding of relationships. They bring with them images of the way things were; and these images may clash with the evolving family system. Also, the losses that all members have experienced must be taken into account. Even though adults and children (teens) have physically separated from one another, the psychological remnants of past relationships tend to linger on for quite some time. This is further complicated by the observation that past adult/teen bonds are now partially altered. These bonds, however, predate the newer relatioships and may pose difficulties.

The absence of a biological parent places a strain on teens as they attempt to negotiate new family roles and expectations. What we see in blended families is the creation of an instant intact-family unit whose members may have some continued moments of guilt, anger, and disappointment. Previous teen/parent ties may prove quite stressful, resulting in a condition that requires immediate attention by all members. However, how can ex-spouses who had problems communicating handle a crisis caused by the merging of a new family? The fact remains that when a biological parent is alive, and possibly in the same community, that influence is certainly felt.

Sometimes the absent parent seems to be worshiped by the teen. The question of loving a new parent can seem disloyal, especially if unresolved feelings still remain. When the biological parents have not resolved their conflicts, it may prove difficult for them to share or enjoy their children. Often these offspring may, knowingly or unknowingly, push the new couple apart. With teens, this may not be the case because of their own developmental concerns with autonomy, although it very well could be a point of tension.

Blended families face still other challenges. Adolescents may feel they are torn between two households. In moving back and forth, teens may be asked to adapt to different routines or ways of doing daily tasks. This is confusing and may provide ammunition for a fight with an adult. Such mundane areas as cleaning up, television or music-listening time and content, going out on dates, curfew, type of clothes—all can be stylistically different from household to household. Teens who are already struggling with identity questions will again ask, "Who am I?" and "Where do I fit in?" They might ask these questions silently but their protest may be expressed in angry actions or by ignoring parents.

The issue of sex in the blended family is a complicated affair. The sexuality of the parent toward the new partner, the sexually based feelings toward stepsiblings, and stepparent/biological-parent conflicts over the sexuality of the teen—all are major areas that could plague young people and family relations.

Finally, the partners themselves may be at different stages of development. As two adults coming together, one may be enmeshed in a career while the other is thinking about having children or being satisfied with home management responsibilities. These families may also have children at various stages of devlopment. A mother, for example, might bring her seven-year-old son, while her new husband could have a thirteen-year-old daughter who may spend only periodic time with them or may actually live in the same household. In some instances these age differences can be useful as an older teen may be able to assume some child-care responsibilities.

Given the concerns in blended families, the specific needs of adults and teens seem obvious. Family members require support, understanding, nurturing, and role clarity. The individuals cannot be forced to look or act like members of a nuclear family, for in reality they are not. Each person's developmental history and needs are different, and therefore all family members need role expectations which fit the place they are in their particular development. Since all households are different, neither teen nor adult should impose previous ways of thinking and acting on the other. Differences in life-styles are not necessarily unhealthy, yet the expectations members place upon one another should be reasonable, in that they acknowledge the individuality of each family member. Understanding and tolerance can be developed through shared activities, such as a weekly meeting. Sometimes the entire family could take part in an activity, while on other occasions the children or parents could do things separately. When family members take time to build new family ties, individuals have the opportunity to gradually break down barriers and become accustomed to the differences each person brings to the new household. Family members have a need to be heard and understood. This is especially critical if parents or teens are moving through difficult developmental transitions. The more relationship building can take place, the more cohesion the members will feel toward one another.

A part of all this is the need of teens to have a link with the biological parent. This will require some type of positive communication between ex-spouses. Rather than place a teen in the middle of a battle between a divorced couple, it is essential that the relationship remain courteous. A working relationship between ex-spouses decreases any feelings of negativism and anxiety a teen may have toward one or the other parent. If there is a problem in a merged family, a divorce mediator can help all parties work it out.

Single Parenthood: Doing It Alone

Single-parent households abound in our contemporary society. In most of these homes, there is a single-parent mother, although the number of single-parent fathers is increasing every day. Major role changes take place when there is a passage from an intact family to a single-parent situation. If a woman has not been working, wage-earning potential becomes an obstacle. She finds she must either return to work or increase her wage-earning capacity; this will mean involvement in an academic curriculum or a job-training program. More stress is placed on the home, since child care may become necessary, or a teen in the home may have to assume this responsibility. Another issue is one of autonomy. Will the overburdened parent "force" the teen to take over absent-parent responsibilities? Or will the teen "experience the world," since no parent is around to stop such misbehavior as skipping school or using drugs. If a father is making the transition to single parenthood, he may need to prepare himself for both child-care and home-management tasks. Frequently a single-parent father may lack skill or confidence in assuming this new role. (Men in intact families continue to take a secondary position in child-rearing areas, so their skills are often untested until a separation or divorce occurs, although this situation seems to be slowly changing.)

Role changes in single-parent homes also involve the relationship between ex-spouses and the children or teenagers in the family. How will the ex-partner relate? What amount of time will be spent between the ex-spouse and the teen? And what type relationship will the teen "set up" with the single parent's male or female friends? These questions pose real stress on single-parent families and are issues that require clear resolution.

Finally, there will be stresses due to the overriding demands of being a single parent. In the intact family, partners may have assumed mutual responsibility for household and community chores, while in the single-parent home all these must be accomplished by one person. Irrespective of any psychological absence of the ex-spouse prior to single-parent status, doing it alone makes a major physical, emotional, and psychological difference. With all this in mind, one wonders how quality time is possible in the single-parent home. If quality interaction occurred within the intact family, then the parent and/or the child(ren) will feel an initial loss. Such interaction is, however, possible, once new roles have been defined for family members and employment opportunities stabilize. The parent will need to take stock of the resources available to carry on leisure-time pursuits. Then both parent and teen can plan activities that fit the family's budget and/or interests.

Role changes and altered expectations may place added strain on each family member, or these changes could help each person regroup and reorder the chaos caused by the transitions. After new roles are defined, quality time can be a goal toward which the family unit works. An important factor in the single-parent home is the teen's relationship with the absent parent. This relationship may also be redefined so that the time spent together can be meaningful.

Dual Career Families: Working with Overload

Dual-career families are quite common in today's world. We see intact families, and blended units as well, with two adult wage earners, when both spouses either want to or need to work. When both husband and wife of an intact family work, the situation may be nonproblematic, depending on how both parents view and schedule their work-worlds with the parenting and adult portions of their lives. The intact family has a patterned way of handling its routines and may have developed extremely efficient negotiating skills in light of the varying needs of each family member. In blended families, working conditions may or may not be problematic, depending on how the styles of both family units mesh. Parents may enter a merged unit with careers already in place, or they may find later that it is necessary for both to work. If the blended family unit has established a compatible set of interactions, then the pressures could be minimized.

However, the dual-career family has stress unique in and of itself. The question of overload is an initial concern for the couple and their offspring. Not only are there household and parenting activities, but the additional interests of a job or career add stress. Whether it is necessary for both parents to work, or there is simply an intense desire to pursue a career, lack of time and energy may create overload. The experience of these families is akin to a highly skilled juggling act; parents feel they are trying to keep several balls in the air simultaneously.

A second stress in dual-career families relates to the adults' perception of themselves as parents, as marriage partners, and as wage earners in their chosen careers. How this question of identity is resolved will have an effect on the relationship between parents and teens. The marital relationship, in which individual and partner needs are met, is critical to the life of the family—the way overall family functioning is played out. Questions of identity also carry over into the adult/teen relationship. If parents are secure in their perception of themselves as partners and as career persons or wage earners, then their relationship with their offspring can be that much more secure and meaningful.

A third stress factor, related to the others, concerns the way parents mesh their career demands with the changing developmental needs of their growing teenagers. The greater stress caused by the additional demands of a two-career household forces parents into finding ways to interact with their teens. Parents can fall into patterns that result in failure to detect a lack of interaction until there is a problem such as cutting school or abusing drugs.

Finding quality time in dual-career families is not impossible. It will mean an intentional changing of noninteractive patterns into a sharing of routine tasks, duties, and leisure time. It also will require both teens and parents to purposely slot-in time for activities that can be enjoyed by the entire family or by two or three. Certain evenings can be planned when all the family members sit down and talk or take part in a special preplanned event.

One family set aside two or three meals a week as special times to be together. The household consisted of an eleven-year-old daughter and two sons, thirteen and fifteen. The father was a doctor, the mother, a schoolteacher. With two teenagers and an active preadolescent, everyone's schedule was hectic, but both parents made it a point that certain meals were mandatory for everyone. During those times, family members could really connect and fill one another in on the week's happenings. There were also meaningful activities outside the home, often planned by all the family members.

Since dual-career families have become a permanent part of family life in our country, it is essential for parents, teens, and younger children to learn how to interact within an overscheduled life-style. Quality time is achieved in these families by the effectiveness of the members' intercommunication. The more open and detailed family members are in sharing information about their personal lives, the more cohesion each individual will feel in the family itself.

Family Types and Family Structures

The reader may recall our discussion of family types in Chapter 1. These included different styles of member-to-member interaction which contributed to the way family members worked for or against achieving quality time. These four family types included cooperative and adversarial, as well as overinvolved and underinvolved structures.

We can observe the contrasts in functioning between adults and teens and sharpen our understanding of these relationships by looking at the following matrix.

Teen and Adult Relationship Matrix

	Cooperative Teen	Adversarial Teen	Overinvolved Teen	Underinvolved Teen
Cooperative Adult	1 + / +	2 + / –	3 + / –	4 + / –
Adversarial Adult	5 – / +	6 – / –	7 – / –	8 – / –
Overinvolved Adult	9 – / +	10 – / –	11 – / –	12 – / –
Underinvolved Adult	13 – / +	14 – / –	15 – / –	16 – / –

How to Use the Teen and Adult Relationship Matrix

In this matrix we can examine both the adult and the teen role, and we can see that, depending upon situational factors, the pattern of family interaction will change. Since everyone must adjust to change, an objective approach to the interaction in a family is the key to reestablishing cooperation and support when a crisis arises.

On the horizontal line at the top of the chart are four descriptions of the teen's role—supportive or cooperative, adversarial, overinvolved, and underinvolved. The vertical column on the left lists the corresponding adult roles. Only those relationships which have either the teen or the adult in the cooperative or supportive role are viewed as growth-oriented. In essence, too much of a good thing may actually limit the growth of either the teen or the adult. This is true when either the teen or the parent is overinvolved. This overinvolvement appears as a compensation for real or perceived inadequacies and probably inhibits normal patterns of development and independence.

You will notice that at times the positions of your family members will appear in different squares of the matrix. All families will be shaken off-balance for a time when a crisis arises. The measure of cohesion within a family is determined by the way its members resolve or react to that crisis. For example, a father might feel that, in general, both he and his teen are cooperative and supportive of one another. But what happens when the father loses his job and takes out his anger on the teenage son—for playing music too loud or letting his hair grow too long? For a time, the father might act and speak in an adversarial way and the teen might react in an adversarial or underinvolved way until the crisis passes. As the father adjusts to the situation by coping with the loss, the hurt feelings, and the fear, or finds new employment, then the family can return to its more positive pattern of relating. We believe that as you read and complete Chapter 6, you will review both the chronic and the situational responses of your family to its experiences. This will provide you with some perspective on how your family functions and what you might do to improve its styles of interaction. In reading the chart, notice that the upper left triangles denote adult roles; the lower right triangles show the corresponding teen roles. The + signs indicate a good relationship; the − signs, a relationship that could be improved. Each of the sixteen combinations warrants a brief explanation.

1. *Cooperative Adult/Cooperative Teen*
   Interaction between family members is functional. Parents and teen are clear in their communication, share household responsibilities, and are understanding of one another's general needs. In this family unit, members are dealing effectively with developmental concerns; they allow one another the growing room needed, not only to feel a part of the family but to see themselves as individuals. Individual needs generally are understood and efforts made to meet them. Major issues of confrontation arise, but are solved through the mutual respect between family members and their ability to discuss problems openly.

2. *Cooperative Adult/Adversarial Teen*
   Interaction here is problematic. The teen in this case may be hostile, uncooperative, and unwilling or unable to share in productive goals because of internal difficulties or external influences—drugs, peers, and so on. In this case the parent is making an effort to deal with the teen; most of the problems are arising from the behavior of the teen.

3. *Cooperative Adult/Overinvolved Teen*
   Here the family's interaction is for the most part very positive. The response on the part of the parents is helpful and oriented toward quality interaction. The teen is willing, possibly overly committed to pleasing the parents or other family members. In such instances, we might observe adolescents who are extremely dependent and passive in asserting themselves in the family and are overly involved in their interaction. Parents may not perceive anything wrong in this situation. Teens may model the parents to a T, yet deny their own preferences or needs, tending to shape desires around parental expectations. If one examined communication and authority here, a high degree of parental control of a more subtle nature would be visible.

4. *Cooperative Adult/Underinvolved Teen*
   Interaction is positive on the parents' part. They demonstrate understanding and patience, and are more or less benign authority figures to the teen.

Teens, on the other hand, may be into their own world, caught up in reacting to their personal development. This adolescent could possibly become withdrawn or isolated and show little interest in family concerns. The parents may be blindly giving too much without requiring the teen to meet responsibilities—that is, carry out household chores. Additionally, parents sell themselves short and have problems establishing limits. They frequently want the teen to be a friend, yet teens, realizing the power of "rejection," are able to hook parents into trying harder to please.

5. *Adversarial Adult/Cooperative Teen*
   Interaction is tense in this system due to the adversarial or negative reactions of the adult, who may be overly critical or experiencing personal probems due to job concerns, drug dependency, or personal issues related to self-development. The teen, in contrast, is cooperative and understanding of the parent's reaction and tries to maintain an open relationship by being sensitive to the needs of the parent. This teen tends to be very dependent and inclined to please the adult. The teen submits to the tyrannical nature of the adult, and at times may feel inadequate and believe punishment is deserved.

6. *Adversarial Adult/Adversarial Teen*
   Interaction in this family system is primarily

negative, with almost no positive interplay between members. We see little if any open communication; family members show a variety of behaviors that undercut one another and move against meeting the needs of individuals. They express almost no positive regard for one another, like gladiators who fight to the death.

7. *Adversarial Adult/Overinvolved Teen*
Here we see a compensatory reaction on the part of the adolescent to a verbally or physically aggressive parent. The teen appears to make up for these negative reactions and may try very hard to cover up the problems of the adult and make excuses for odd behaviors. In addition, the teen is unable to express anger for many of the parent's inappropriate actions but will try to please, no matter how unreasonable the parent.

8. *Adversarial Adult/Underinvolved Teen*
In this family system, the parent is typically critical or experiencing some personal problem which causes negative reactions to family members. The teen, in response, may retreat or become withdrawn from the family unit. The teen generally lacks the energy or interest to become involved and seems detached or distant. The adolescent may feel overwhelmed or defeated by the attitude of the adult and strike out on his or her own. Friends become more important than family members.

9. *Overinvolved Adult/Cooperative Teen*
   In this family the parents seem very concerned and involved in the lives of their offspring. At times they become overprotective and continue to take over responsibilities that the teen could normally pursue. The teen who is cooperative allows the parent to be overprotective without a negative response. Here the adolescent shows an ability to differentiate and maintain a sense of individuality, in spite of the parent's overprotectiveness, and frequently can express feelings about the relationship. The teen in this case shows a high level of understanding and maturity.

10. *Overinvolved Adult/Adversarial Teen*
    Here the parent is intrusive and overprotective about the issues of the teen. The adolescent reacts in an adversarial manner to the exaggerated needs of the parent with negative, uncommunicative, and insensitive behavior both in and away from the home. The parent in this instance seems overly engaged in the life of the teen, having not yet resolved his or her own issues. The teen apparently is developing as expected socially, emotionally, and cognitively.

11. *Overinvolved Adult/Overinvolved Teen*
    The reaction of the adult is met equally by the teen, who becomes hooked into the system and overidentifies with the protective nature of the parent's behavior. In this enmeshed relationship, a dependency and helplessness may develop on

the teen's part. Both teen and adult anchor to the family unit and neglect outside contacts.

12. *Overinvolved Adult/Underinvolved Teen*
Again the parents are highly protective and more interested in teen issues than in their own life concerns. These teens tend to move away from attempts of the parents to stifle their individuality; they distance themselves from their families by locking into a private world and refusing to meet the responsibilities of the family unit. A teen might manipulate the parent, receiving allegiance even when the parent should disengage (e.g., chronic delinquency).

13. *Underinvolved Adult/Cooperative Teen*
Here we have a parent who cannot fulfill expected household duties and has difficulty providing emotional support to the family. A divorced mother may be temporarily unable to meet the normal demands within the household. The teen, on the other hand, may be able to pick up the slack and take over certain responsibilities. An interesting point here is that teens may not respond this way in their relationship with absent fathers; they can play a different role with fathers. This can occur in an intact family as well.

14. *Underinvolved Adult/Adversarial Teen*
The parent's uninvolved response is met by the adversarial reaction of the teen. Here the adolescent may be responding to the parent or may be demonstrating adversarial or conflictual

behavior because of input from peers, drugs, or other community factors. The parent in this case seems detached and overly concerned about self or career interests. The teen attempts to obtain parental nurturing in negative ways.

15. *Underinvolved Adult/Overinvolved Teen*
An uninvolved parent response in either household or emotional/affectional areas is met by the compensatory reaction of the teen, who tries to make up for the parent's inability to function effectively. In this instance, however, the adolescent also overreacts and, in doing so, is unable to meet individual needs. Outside-the-home interests are neglected.

16. *Underinvolved Adult/Underinvolved Teen*
This final category concerns an underinvolved adult and an equally underinvolved teen who may be modeling the behaviors of the parent or experiencing personal issues related to adolescence. This situation detracts from the teen's ability to feel a part of the family situation.

These categories assume a relationship between a parent and a teen. However, the situation becomes much more complex when one considers the multiple possibilities. In a two-parent home, one parent might play an adversarial, an overprotective, or an undersupportive role, while the other parent does not. The interaction between the pair may cause further difficulty in the teen/parent relationship. Parents who relate to each other in nonproductive or conflictual ways can expect a negative effect upon their relationship with their children. Therefore it is essential that parents understand and assess their relationship to each other, to help bring about a more mutually satisfying emotional tone between themselves and their teen.

In contrast to a cooperative family life-style, one might visualize an intact adversarial family unit. Here, even without the strain of an altered family condition, the adversarial tone would impede the amount of quality time that could evolve. The relationships of family members, adults and teen(s) alike, would show the following patterns:

—a sense of dominance and control, especially between parents and teens
—undefined parent/teen boundaries; each person is unsure of his/her role
—inability to negotiate or establish a set of family goals
—lack of responsibility for behavior; others are blamed for one's inappropriate actions
—limited ability to openly express feelings that would have a direct bearing on the developmental concerns of family members
—little or no ability to resolve conflicts or differences between family members.

The sixteen categories also are not necessarily exclusive, as there may be a certain amount of carryover from one combination to another. The type of family interaction will affect the family's structure, just as the strains on a family affect the tone of that family's interaction. In other words, there seems to be a direct relationship between these two conditions. For example, a single-parent family might have developed a cooperative life-style. Role changes, or a redefinition of the way the parent and teen run their daily lives, could be accomplished in a cooperative manner. Quality time in this case would be attained by the willingness of parent and teen to build the following kind of relationship:

—a closeness, but with clear personal boundaries between teen and adult
—a decision-making process that is negotiable, depending upon the age of the teen and the parent's willingness
—a clarity of ideas and thoughts
—responsibilities that are willingly assumed by family members
—privacy that is allowed to varying degrees
—receptiveness to the ideas of the other person(s) in the family
—resolution of conflict issues
—sensitivity to one another's life situations.

With this style of interaction, the pressures that might normally bear upon a one-parent family (or any family system) could be greatly diminished.

Special Issues to Consider

In altered family systems, we note that certain basic issues are more relevant than others. In single-parent homes, the degree of autonomy between parent and teen, communication style, development of a self-identity, the amount of closeness experienced by family members—all are most important issues.

A mother who was divorced when her son was twelve has remained single and now dates periodically, while her son, now sixteen, has just received his driver's license. His autonomy has increased, as was expected. The mother is handling this quite well and realizes the need for her son's growing independence. (Being able to drive helps provide independence.) Although she deals with the issue of autonomy on a somewhat relaxed level, the mother is vaguely uncomfortable when she thinks about her single status and her son's increased movement away from the home, an expected turn of events with which she must cope.

This example is significant in light of the other variables which need careful attention in a single-parent household. Communication needs to be open and clear as both parent and teen deal with their own developmental needs. Family members must work also toward a clearer definition of role, or self-identity, as each struggles with personal life concerns. Finally, parents and teens in this kind of family should examine how closely aligned each wants and needs to be with the other. There must be a balance between becoming too involved and too removed, when it comes to parent/teen relationships in a single-parent unit. This is also relevant when making decisions about the relationship between the ex-spouse and the teenager.

Blended families may have similar issues with which to contend, yet their situation is certainly different from that of the single-parent home. Merged families must consider the internal power. When two families are brought together, their styles of leadership in dealing with one another may not be the same. Who has control in the family? Who gets who to carry out household chores? Who has the final say between different sets of children? All these questions must be considered, and there must be consistency in leadership, to define agreed-upon rules by which all can live.

Since family members bring their own histories into a new unit, parents and teens need to show one another a degree of empathy; an understanding of how the others might feel because of the family situation from which each has come. It will help if both sets of parent/teen(s) have made the transition from an intact to a blended situation, but this is only a starting point. Therefore, to better understand the differences that exist, communication should remain open and constant if at all possible. Finally, blended family members need to be aware of one another's personal space. Each person has the right to privacy and at times needs to be alone. Respect for one another's possessions, emotions, and physical space is therefore essential.

Dual-career families also face certain issues that warrant our attention. First, there should be a willingness to negotiate the questions of scheduling and work overload. Family members will develop stronger, more meaningful relationships if they understand and accept the demands placed on the household because of the dual responsibilities of parents. Resentments should be explored and agreements set up so that teens and parents alike not only realize the stresses placed upon the family, but are also aware of the rewards and leisure-time possibilities that can be gained. In spite of the highly demanding schedules, quality time can be an attainable and workable goal.

These examples illustrate the way families play out their lives together, given the stresses within the family units as compared to the nature of the members' interaction. When thinking about quality time, it is important to understand your place in the family matrix. Once that has been determined, decisions can be made as to how family members can best live together, as this reflects the relationship issues between teen and parent. In Chapter 4 we will illustrate certain problem areas more extensively.

CHAPTER 4

At-Risk Families: Pitfalls for Teens and Parents

We have discussed the characteristics of families by identifying the connection between family type and family structure. By portraying this as a matrix, families can begin to note their interactional position in this two-dimensional framework. As we have seen, the nature of teen/parent interaction can be greatly complicated by the different family structures that are becoming commonplace in many American communities. Quality time is, in turn, affected by the very nature of the interaction, so it is important to examine the areas of the matrix that are problematic—the areas that signal the at-risk factors confronting many families today.

At-Risk Points in the Teen/Parent Relationship

When parents and teens have honestly acknowledged their style of interacting, some determination can be made as to the direction the relationship could take. The at-risk areas on the matrix are noted by the degree of over- or underinvolvement on the part of the parent or the teen. Adversarial reactions on the part of parent or teen, of course, are also problematic and signify an arrangement that is less than growth producing, one in which quality time becomes more difficult to achieve. What frequently happens is that either the parent or the teen responds to the other in a way that implies a negative reaction to a situation. When such a reaction occurs, the relationship between family members is colored by the fact that certain individual needs are not being met or that one member is compensating for some part of the relationship that may be perceived as missing.

An examination of the matrix reveals that many of the cells in the table may result in situations that are problematic. Generally, when either the teen or the parent is cooperative, however, conflict issues that normally develop can be minimized. The more at-risk conditions arise when we consider categories 6, 7, 8, 10, 11, 14, 15, and 16. Each of these represents a style of interaction that diminishes the esteem of a family member or impedes the potential of family members to meet their individual needs.

Certain family situations bring about a greater sense of alarm than others. These might include teen behaviors such as:

—drug use
—poor academic performance
—unwanted pregnancy

—running away from home
—breaking curfew
—withdrawal and potential suicidan behavior.

In a similar fashion, the problematic behaviors of parents might include:
—marital conflict and discord
—heavy use of alcohol or drugs
—neglect of parental responsibilities
—irresponsibility in job or career.

Examples of the way some of these different behaviors are either initiated or escalated by the adversarial and under- or overinvolved reactions of parents or teens will give a clearer understanding of at-risk situations in families.

Drug Use

In our society, both teens and parents can become chemically dependent upon either drugs or alcohol. Commonly, teens, viewing their own peer culture, begin to experiment with alcohol or with a variety of drugs. For parents and teens this can become a critical time which may place the entire family in jeopardy. Unfortunately, many teens see their parents also misusing alcoholic beverages or other substances, and this gives teens a further license to experiment on their own.

For purposes of our discussion, however, we will assume that parents need to assess their response to their teen's use of alcohol or drugs. Certainly the parent can control the use of these substances in the home, but has little if any control over their use in the community. Thus the parental question: How do I respond to my teenager when I suspect that he or she is using drugs? The answer lies in not becoming an at-risk family. Or, if your family is already at risk, in doing something about it.

At-risk families, in this instance, will respond in an adversarial, overprotective, or undersupportive fashion. Again, by looking at the categories in Chapter 3, one can see that any one of these responses may only drive the teen further into drug experimentation. An adversarial parent will be hostile, challenging, unwilling to listen, imposing, and domineering. An *overinvolved* parent may become highly involved, intrusive, overprotective, and smothering, willing to assume most of the responsibilities that should be given to the teen. *Underinvolved* responses also cause difficulties: The parents may be detached or nonattending, pulling away, not interested in becoming involved in their teen's life. This is a cue to adolescents that they are allowed complete freedom with no limits whatsoever. For instance:

Richard is sixteen. His mother, a single parent, has created an extremely close symbiotic bond with her son. One afternoon while he is in school, she finds a bag of marijuana under the couch in the living room. When Richard comes home, his mother overreacts. She screams, yells, and gives him the "third degree," demanding to know where the drugs came from.

Richard is defensive. He denies the marijuana is his—he claims it was dropped there by friends. His mother however, keeps insisting that he is involved with drugs and that she does not know what to do with him.

Similar examples probably occur in many homes across America. The bag of marijuana may actually belong to Richard. But by reacting as she does, his mother only heightens his defensiveness, pushing him further into the drug culture of which he may already be a part. She does not listen to explanations but becomes overreactive and is viewed by her son as being very intrusive in his life. Richard's mother, of course, is not pleased to find drugs in her home, but she could respond in a less critical, attacking manner. Her response alienates Richard, pushing him further away from home.

This condition of being distanced from the parent(s) is not unusual for many young people in numerous high schools throughout the United States. Since drug use occurs on a variety of levels, parents, before overreacting, should assess how deeply involved their teen is. For example, are the drugs left around for you to find because the teen wants more of your time and attention? The reaction of one or both parents complicates the issue. Both teens and parents should be concerned about the affect of drugs on the functioning of the family and on the way family members react to one another. This will be a critical factor in resolving the question of chemical dependency.

School Performance

There are two categories of problems having to do with school performance. One concerns difficulties based on learning disabilities as assessed by professionals—school psychologists and special education personnel. The second category includes problems caused by not attending class, talking back to teachers, and cutting school.

For many teens and parents, school performance and academic achievement can be major sources of conflict. Parents who are adversarial or oversupportive and highly involved in the life of a teen tend to continually question what the teen is doing or not doing in school. Other parents behave in a detached manner. They are so self-involved that they are unwilling or unable to show interest in the teen's work at school. These parents often ignore a professional recommendation to seek therapy and, in essence, deny their parental involvement—they blame the teen or the school. The following example illustrates one teen's struggle to perform well in a school setting.

Dave's thirteen-year-old son, Harrison, has had difficulty in school for several years. Assessed as learning disabled, he has been placed in a special class. Dave, who has a Ph.D, sees Harrison as not functioning satisfactorily. His grades are poor and he frequently runs away from school and returns home. Dave has reacted to his son's problem by becoming adversarial and detached. Harrison has not received any emotional support in his work at school and has developed an adversarial and alienated attitude toward both school and his father. Thus a hostile relationship has developed between Dave and Harrison.

Frequently a parent's indifference or alienation, which may have been building for years, will cause an adverse reaction and ineffective behavior. On the other hand, schools and classroom teachers may not be able to provide the impetus a teen so desperately needs in order to digest the educational material being offered. This, in combination with the fact that a teen is distracted by peers, drugs, music, and so on, complicates the matter. This kind of situation creates an at-risk condition for the family, in that a particular need of one of its members is not being met.

Unwanted Pregnancy

We know that each year, about 1.3 million young women between the ages of thirteen and eighteen become pregnant. These out-of-wedlock pregnancies cause the teens and their families tremendous stress. Some teenagers decide to keep their babies, but the majority make alternative plans: They may choose abortion or decide to place the child for adoption. Whatever decision is made, however, generally causes both teen and parent much anxiety and confusion.

The nature of the parents' response to this situation will usually determine the degree of conflict in the home. If a parent tends to react in an adversarial fashion, the end result usually will be a high level of dysfunction in the family, especially if the teen responds adversarially. Parents who are very critical and negative about the pregnancy cause the daughter to react by withdrawing from, or even escaping the family environment. In fact, in cases where the home environment has been adversarial, it is not unusual for a teenager to develop other social relationships, later finding herself with an unwanted pregnancy. Young women who have been experiencing an adversarial relationship with one of their parents will, in all likelihood, be fearful of disclosing the fact that they are pregnant. Many will seek other options and find ways of not having the child.

The nature of the relationship between the adolescent and the parent will determine the amount of openness and sharing during this crisis, so that a rational, acceptable decision can be made.

Breaking of Curfew

All situations in family life are not of crisis proportions. The breaking of curfew is a normal happening in the lives of most teens. When limits are set at an appropriate level for an adolescent's age, curfew times will frequently be adhered to. If parents overreact to an occasional breaking of curfew without substantial reason, then they will meet with constant resistance. A case in point makes this quite clear:

Charles is sixteen, an attractive, bright, yet manipulative youngster who has problems at school and at home. Many of his difficulties are, unfortunately, related to his mother, who is constantly "on his case." She watches his every move and has become generally intrusive in his life. One Saturday evening, Charles tells his parents he is going to a party at a certain person's house. At 10 o'clock, his mother calls the party to ask Charles some information she needs, but finds that Charles never arrived. Frantic, the mother searches the neighborhood streets, calling his name; eventually she gives up the search and returns home. When Charles learns from friends that his mother has tried to locate him, he becomes quite angry.

This incident proved embarrassing to Charles. He has been pushed to his limit by a parent who, for several years, has acted in a highly intrusive manner. In addition, she has been unable to set appropriate limits. Charles' behavior has become manipulative and inconsistent, a partial result of the pattern of interaction between the two. The mother has involved herself in her son's life, at the same time denying herself the opportunity to develop her own interests.

In this at-risk situation, the individuals are not meeting their own needs because of the behavior of each toward the other. Charles has reacted to the situation by becoming extremely troublesome and at times adversarial, characteristics that might have been mitigated by a more cooperative family environment. Perhaps this family could solve its problem by entering therapy, with the purpose of freeing both mother and teen so that each could live a more appropriate life.

Suicidal Actions

Teenage suicide may represent the ultimate in at-risk conditions for parents and teens. We know that adolescent suicide has been increasing over the past three years. The reasons have been given much attention. Generally, causal factors range from feelings of emptiness and aimlessness to an overriding sense of anomie or normlessness, in addition to an overall void in bonding with family or peers. Another critical variable may be related to teens' lack of self-identity, which emerges slowly during this period, yet is an essential piece in the life-style the adolescent chooses to enact. Without this emerging image of self based on accomplished acts or skills which the teen believes he or she has attained, the personhood the adolescent so desperately needs will be negatively impacted.

Teens who give any indication of desire to end their lives frequently have been members of an at-risk family unit. Undersupportive or adversarial parent reaction can contribute greatly to teens' feelings of hopelessness about their life direction. Although suicidal gestures can manipulate oversupportive parents into action, it is important that parents not overlook or deny the actions or words of teens who threaten to end their lives. The following case is not unusual today:

At age ten, Thomas was sent by his mother to live with his father in another town. The father was heavily into drugs, as were most of the other relatives with whom he associated, and Thomas was allowed to use a variety, from marijuana to angel dust. His early and middle adolescence were experienced in a haze. Adolescence passed him by; an emergent identity never took hold. He saw himself as an empty shell of a person. Thomas was sixteen when family and individual counseling began. He had been hospitalized for severe depression and attempted suicide. After leaving the hospital, and now back with his mother and younger sister, he was successful in staying away from drugs for long periods of time, but continued to do poorly in school in spite of above-average intelligence. He had constant feelings of anxiety and rejection, and repeatedly stayed away from home, either with his girlfriend or with other classmates. Finally, at seventeen, Thomas committed suicide.

By examining the interactional categories in Chapter 3, we can identify the at-risk situation in Thomas' case: an undersupportive mother and father who could not establish defined limits for his behavior. Thomas was sent to his father because his mother was centered on some of her own needs at that time. Thomas perceived this as rejection and believed that his father's casual attitude toward drugs was a license to do as he pleased.

These undersupportive behaviors indicate the parents' low level of emotional commitment, along with their detachment and disregard for Thomas' general welfare. This was a partial cause of his limited identity, poor feeling of self-worth, and hopeless attitude toward the future.

The examples we have discussed in this chapter represent at-risk family situations. Countless others might have been cited. Frequently teens and adults need professional help to untangle the chaos that exists in their families. The decision as to whether the adolescent or other family members require intervention from a professional counselor should be based on the severity of interaction in the home and the length of time that condition has existed. At-risk families can be helped if there is a desire for change within the family system.

Difficult Family Moments

In spite of professional assistance, certain family members will be unable to cope or adjust. When reactions of teen or adult are extreme over a period of time—that is, adversarial and conflicted, underinvolved or detached, overextended or enmeshed, other questions should be raised. Do certain persons feel they are to blame for this situation? And how long can a family hang on to a member who is not improving or not willing to receive help? Sometimes individuals are so caught up in their own concerns or encumbered with critical emotional or psychological problems that they cannot function within the family unit. In such a case, a family would do well to inquire about getting help for the person who has impaired his or her own growth as well as the potential growth of other family members. Frequently this type of decision is extremely difficult and uncomfortable—even to the point that individuals will resist asking for assistance and try to cover up or deny a situation that may be tearing relationships apart, or at least preventing them from being strengthened.

Family dysfunction often can be linked to established patterns of family behavior—behavior that obviously would be unproductive in bringing about a sense of family solidarity and cohesion. On the other hand, individuals who have weakened opinions about their own worth can create conflicted relationships with others in the family. Examine your own family interaction and make an attempt to avoid the following major characteristics of an at-risk family:

1. *Inability to see family members as individuals in their own right.* Obviously, adversarial, overinvolved, or underinvolved families would tend to have difficulty adjusting to developmental and life-stage changes. The inability to see the individual as a separate person often leads teen or parent to destructive or noncooperative activities. At best, there is an inability to perceive accurately the actions and words of others.

2. *A high degree of alcohol or substance abuse, with inability to control behavior.* This condition tends to lead to either underinvolved or adversarial parenting. The chemically dependent person might also, when not high on chemicals, be overly involved or attempt to "make up" for drink or drug-related behavior. This pendulum swing often confuses the teen, who learns not to trust the "good" behavior and remembers only the negative experiences. This can result in blocked interpersonal communication between teen and parent.

3. *Physical or verbal abuse which becomes a patterned response for family members in handling their personal frustrations and problems.* This may result in either the teen or the parent becoming adversarial or detached from the family. Here family members could become involved in promiscuity, drug use, gambling, or other self-destructive activities.

4. *Chronic failure in school or in job performance, with inability to openly assess one's own responsibilities.* People can internalize a sense of failure and feel ashamed or guilty. A sense of unworthiness pushed inward becomes self-deprecating. As a result, the individual may pull away from other family members. In contrast, an adversarial reaction is not uncommon—here people project their feelings onto others and ridicule others for their own failure.

5. *Unwillingness to listen to the concerns of other family members.* Family members who are adversarial and underinvolved would have difficulty "hearing" other persons. Not listening sets up an adverse reaction—individuals begin to pull away; they feel nobody really cares about what they think or believe.

6. *Inability to make reasonable or mature choices—a situation that affects family routine and function.* In this case, individuals do not solve problems or negotiate effectively, the result of adversarial, detached, or overinvolved interaction—they are more concerned about their own personal needs than about the needs of others.

7. *Maintenance of extremely rigid family rules and roles, without the willingness to reconsider the needs of the family or of individuals.* In this situation there is an extreme reaction to the way the family and its members carry out functions or tasks. When a family, for example, is dogmatic about religious practices, or does not deviate in any way from the hour everyone must sit down to dinner, an inflexible style of relating to one another is established. This limits the potential growth of individuals in the family.

8. *Inability to give one another the appropriate space or privacy each person needs.* Families that appear adversarial or overinvolved may constrict the normal behavior of members. People are pushed away from interacting in a positive

fashion, and this only "fuels the fire" for more conflicted relations.

9. *Inability or refusal to use or establish positive contact with resources in the surrounding community.* Such families are isolated from a social network offered by religious and educational community services, and/or social interaction with friends and extended family. This style of detachment can be either adversarial ("Those damn teachers can't control this kid!"), overinvolved (an enmeshed family that "handles" teenage chemical abuse *without* professional assistance), or underinvolved (a family that ignores chronic spouse abuse and maintains a detached reaction to this pattern).

Certainly this is not an exhaustive list. Although other qualities of at-risk families could have been added, it is essential that the above be considered when parent and teen reflect upon the nature of their relationship. However, it it not necessary that a family demonstrate all these qualities to be seen as "at risk." Any one or a combination of these elements can prove a detriment to positive interaction. Ultimately, significant and meaningful relationships are developed by accurately perceiving where people are and where they want to be. Unless at-risk families give immediate attention to these trouble spots, positive gains are slow to come about.

CHAPTER 5

Building Bridges: Spanning the Generation Gap

In Chapter 2, we discussed ways parents can show they understand both their own and their teens' life-stage adjustments. Parents, by virtue of their experience, may be in an opportune position to provide objective feedback to teens. This demands that a parent aim for the role of participant-observer. In the case of two-parent families, the adults can help each other gain insight into the quality of their interaction with their child, no matter what the family type.

You might ask, "How can an adult help minimize the long-term negative impact of an adversarial relationship?" We have a great deal of empathy for the parent who realizes and attempts to come to terms with the cause of the problem. Parents who are overly dependent, who need their teens to parent or nurture them, are also in a self-critical role. Parents and significant adults in the lives of teens should honestly evaluate the way both they and the teen are handling their own social, emotional, cognitive, physical, and spiritual development.

Here there is a paradox that the adult must face and resolve: the reality that the teen is becoming an adult and moving toward a complete sense of independence, free of the jurisdiction of the parent. Adolescents ultimately are free to act on their own values, choices, and morals. This presents a dilemma for parents to which there is no clear-cut answer or course of action. This chapter offers a coherent sense of direction for evaluating and maximizing the quality of the relationship, and the love, between parents and teens.

General Guidelines

There is conflict in all human interaction. Perhaps the characteristic that distinguishes one family type from another is not merely the number of conflicts found within a family, but rather the way conflicts and potential conflicts are prevented and resolved before great distance is created between parent and child, or between spouses. Moreover, a cooperative family might be an intact family, but this is not a requirement. Both single-parent and merged families have the potential, and often the quality, of cooperative interaction.

There are some basic characteristics possessed by families whose members function well together in attempting to overcome difficulties. The following list is not complete, but attempts to include the major areas of interaction found in those homes:

1. *Respect for one another is felt and communicated* between parent and child, based on love, affection, appreciation, caring, and responsibility. Love is not based on the fear that it will be taken away and that punishment will result, or on the threat of rejection and denial of the value family members place on one another.

2. *There is a respect between parent and teen in terms of their involvement in their social worlds.* As the teen encounters both success and failure within the peer group and with members of the opposite sex, the adult is available as teacher, comforter, and consultant, or simply as a concerned parent unable to completely shield the child from the realities of life.

3. *There is an emotional maturity that tends to foster a cooperative spirit of interaction* and is appropriate to the life-stage development of both parent and teen. Within the family that has problems (alcohol or physical abuse) the parent might act inappropriately or be more dependent. If the child is always forced to assume family responsibilities—the rearing of younger siblings or the preparation of family meals—both parent and child will be negatively affected in their emotional development. The degree of emotional imbalance will vary depending on the family type, but will also depend on the current level of stress on family members. The loss of a job, discovery of a health problem, or the

impending move of a child from home to college might create an emotional uproar within the family system. Within the cooperative family, there will also be stress, but the ability to communicate feelings, accept the loss, and resolve the adjustment will not block long-term relating. In short, the family members will assume new relationships that do not heavily burden any one person.

4. *Both parent and teen accept any limitations or gifts associated with intellectual ability.* Many children have a greater opportunity for education today. Within the cooperative family, parents will not belittle themselves for their own lack of formal training or worship the gifts their child may have developed naturally or gained through a modern education. There should also be agreement between parents that they will not reinforce competition by comparing siblings who rival for their approval. They should control their reactions at report-card time and their comments to extended family members and friends.

5. *There is an acceptance of the limits that time and life-style have set on our physical abilities.* Parent and child might engage in physical activity as part of a health regimen, but if maintenance of a youthful appearance and stamina are overemphasized or a means of

competition, a cooperative family system could become competitive.

For example, one father's physical ability was always a source of enjoyment to him, as well as a way to gain social acceptance. He had been a teen All-star in both football and basketball. His son was also competitive. When the father and son played one-on-one basketball, both fought hard to win, and eventually, the son beat the father. This defeat was a bitter pill for the father—the physical activity had been more than a game or a skill. He felt his personhood was somehow on the line. Nonetheless, in this instance, the father would have been wiser to work through his need to dominate his son.

In such a severely competitive relationship, a son can't wait for the day he can physically assert himself over his father. Many angry moments may end with the son threatening the father and the father saying, "I'm ready to take you on, Son!" Adolescence is the time the battle is fought, and sometimes lost, by both father and teen.

6. *Parents assist their offspring in becoming aware of their Judeo-Christian heritage* by exposing them to the ideas contained in their religious texts. In today's family, there are too many adults who diligently send their offspring to a place of worship. Some may even accompany them, but few live the teachings of their faith to the fullest extent. It is not that most

parents are hypocrites, but too many seem to lean on a philosophy of do as I say, not as I do!

Within the cooperative family framework, the task of setting spiritual values in the lives of children is a cardinal requirement for proper preparation before entering the contemporary world. The world these teens inherit is overrun with values and questions that most holy books could not have addressed, since the questions did not exist at the time of their origin. For example, how would your teen handle the question of the legal right to life for a child conceived in a laboratory, if its donor father died before its birth? Should the lawful wife of the male donor be allowed to raise the child if the father is dead? Do the unborn have any rights of survivorship?

What questions has your teen raised lately?

It is beyond the scope of this book to answer these moral issues. However, the complexity of these queries hammers home the point that parents can be meaningfully involved with their teens only by establishing a cooperative relationship. If you have gone to religious meetings with your teen, have discussed the critical issues of morality and emphasized their importance in conducting our lives, and have set a consistently good model, then you can say you have tried to teach your child to live by the best possible ideals that religion has set down for us.

However, a teen has free choice. In spite of your moral teaching, your child may choose to rebel. Even though you have set clear limits—that is, no drinking or drug use—this may not prevent your teen from engaging in these acts outside your home. We will acquire a clearer understanding of the reasons for this rebellion as other, more concrete issues are addressed.

Issues of Authority

In order to bridge differences between teens and parents, conflict areas must be identified. Battle lines are drawn over problems with communication, respect for authority, and the ability to love and respect others. Too often people chant the Commandment that children should honor their mothers and fathers. Parents feel their children owe them that respect blindly. However, a major idea in our contemporary world is that no one—no authority by virtue of its title or role—is respected automatically. Granted, parents and other authority figures (teachers, religious leaders, police, scientists) should be respected, but in today's social climate this is not always the case. Those in charge need to be able to relate to teens by better understanding of the teen perception of the world. In order to reach teens, adults must offer a different perspective from the seemingly overwhelming snare of escapist time-consumers such as television, music, and drugs.

What does it mean to be an authority figure in the life of a teen? In the first place, we need to define *authority.* First, authority can be "legislated" into the teen relationship. For example, teachers, police, relatives, and parents are, to some extent, given authority by society. Teachers are responsible for what happens to the teens in their care within the context of the school experience. If students roam out to a grassy knoll on the school property and smoke marijuana, the school officials are held accountable. What do they do? They tackle the problem by teaching about drugs, taking daily attendance, and cooperating with the police if a drug problem is severe enough.

The parental role is akin to the teacher's role. In fact, one could say that parents are the primary teachers and models for teens. In a child's early years, parents appear to radiate significant effect on behaviors and values. In the teen years, other things become more important. Friends and rock heroes provide the idols or experience that fuels the many actions of the adolescent. Though a parent is free from the sin of hiding behind the false philosophy—do as I say, not as I do—a teen might still rebel against the perceived inflexible stance of parents, teachers, and the values learned in earlier years. Second, the authority issue needs to be understood in light of the fact that the parent-child role is a changing one and that flexibility directs the course of action. How else could a parent show compassion for the ambivalence the teen will exhibit in terms of responsibility?

Suppose a teenager had overslept and was late for work. Her mother refused to call in an excuse to the girl's boss. The teen argued, but slowly rose to dress and half-heartedly "volunteered" to call that she would be late. The parent agreed but, in error, made the call herself. Thus the parent would have bailed the teen out by not allowing her to be independent and face the consequences of being late for work.

Communication

The root of all anger is couched in communication problems, whether we consider nations, spouses, or parents and teens. Perhaps the most direct way to improve communication with your teen is to acknowledge that parents communicate best when they see and value their child as a person. When we see our offspring as emerging young men or women, then verbally and by our actions, we will demonstrate cooperative family interaction. In this way we can create an environment in which a teen can model appropriate adult behaviors. If we interact with love and respect, we make it possible (but not automatic) that our teens will treat us with love. Our children, as emerging adults, need compassion. Teens may begin a discussion with respect for their parents, but lose it in the heat of argument. As a parent, you could feel self-righteously abused and unfairly accused. But the more objective position is to remember that teens may "not know what they do" to their parents. If all of us were required to act and speak perfectly on all occasions in order to merit love and respect, none of us would make it!

We believe that effective communication can and often does take place during the course of normal daily routines and can be used to improve quality time.

Quality Time and Communication

How can modern families begin to relate more effectively to their teens on a daily basis? The modern family is not like the Waltons. Most people don't live in a "Little House on the Prairie." And after divorce, families don't easily blend into a "Brady Bunch." In fact, many contemporary families are tied up in a fast-paced, complex set of roles. The parents generally are continually on duty; only occasionally do their roles permit rest. Children are busy, too—in school, on the street; playing, taking lessons. Where parents and children do cross paths, too often the television set is in the intersection, blocking communication.

Communication, effective or ineffective, can either enhance or block the building of a relationship. If a parent asks, "What did you do today at school?" a child usually replies, "Nothing."

You, the parent, could react in a number of ways. You might say, "Sounds something like my job. All I do is nothing."

A more supportive response would be, "Sounds as though you're bored with school." Even if your offspring isn't bored, your words attempt to label the child's feelings.

A child who is not bored might try to clarify your attempt: "No, but I think school is stupid. The teacher is always talking about stupid things."

The next move is yours in this human chess match. If you come back with something like a preachy lecture on the merits of a liberal arts education, you've lost it. A more engaging response addresses the child's view of the world: "When I was in school, I felt the same way. But I learned I was better off when I paid attention, took notes, and answered questions."

"Yes, but sometimes I almost fall asleep."

"Okay, but the teacher can't always be boring and the work can't always be stupid."

The next few bits of the parent's dialogue are a crucial measure of the relationship, judged by how well the parent knows the child. Can you cite a few examples when Johnny or Janey was turned on by the teacher or by a particular subject? If you think you really know your child, then you should be able to name a few positive school experiences.

This type of conversation builds bridges between child and adult. The only barriers that will remain are those between the child and the outside world. The adult can be seen as being on the child's side, rather than as an enemy or a know-it-all.

All persons need to have the important people in their lives listen to them, but pressures on both parents and children tend to limit intimacy. While it is easy to say that quality time should be spent with children, few experts would even try to offer a minute/hour cost-effective formula to manage this part of building a parent/child relationship.

There is an art and a science to relating within the family. But the guiding light to carry a parent through the adventure of parenting is quite simple: Give of yourself. In most cases, children with behavior problems improve when their mothers and fathers spend time with them. An amazing new relationship often blossoms from short personal talks before, during, and after meals, for as little as twenty minutes a day.

Family meetings on a weekly basis can create good family memories and lessons, too. It's not hard to remember that the advertising slogan Reach Out and Touch Someone means being connected to someone we love.

Throwing a ball back and forth hasn't gone out of style or lost its appeal, either. And the magic of hearing a story still can help liberate the imagination of a TV-addicted child. The Waltons and the Bradys zoom into our eyes with the speed of light. Their messages about love, listening, and life are etched into our memories when we watch them and hear them talking together. But wouldn't it be more valuable to spend quality time with your own family?

Could a weekly meeting be held on a regular basis to bond your family together? Can you spare twenty minutes to talk individually with the most important people in your world? A little attention goes a long way in preventing problems or in working them out.

Love and Respect

If life has one meaning that encompasses the complexities of contemporary living, it is that humans can experience love. With the pressure of daily routines and the sometimes difficult life with a teenager, it is a great accomplishment for two people to know and feel love for each other. Too often, we are not very successful at sharing our love. Both teenagers and adults need to reexperience the love they feel for one another. Since life is filled with a seemingly unending series of changes, one responsibility of parents is to demonstrate their love for the teenager in their lives.

Note that the parent is responsible for initiating this exchange, for a number of reasons. First, to some extent, the teen is embroiled in the difficulties of a significant rite of passage. The parents may be just as mired, but at least have lived through their teen years and should take responsibility for their own life adjustments. In addition, parents should give love first, in order to receive love from their child. Third, parents must objectively understand the pattern of the way love and respect have been exchanged with their teen. If they have not taught their child how to love and show respect, both parents and teen are losers. Fourth, parents need to know and understand their teen in a total developmental way. As defined in *Real Men Enjoy Their Kids* (Singer, Shechtman, Singer [Abingdon Press, 1983]), they must look at the social, emotional, cognitive, physical, and spiritual levels of development in their child, see and accept their teen as an individual who is separate and unique. This is the goal that best serves their child's growth.

Last, we need to look at ourselves as individuals along those same dimensions of total growth (for none of us ever really finishes growing). Each life stage presents an opportunity for us to know the world in a more complete way. None of us is close enough to perfection to swagger down the lane as a self-possessed guru, thinking ourself better than all other people. For at a very basic level, we all have been given gifts or potentials and are challenged to reach for our "stars." But no one can be a star in every possible way. If you can see your child in this reasonable fashion, you can give both yourself and your teen the space you need in order to grow. No one could ask more of parents than that they love and teach their child the values that lead to a successful, happy, fulfilling life.

Changes Affecting Teens and Parents

There are both internal and external factors that shade the way teens see the world. The adolescent "make up" determines how and to what extent parents can implement a relationship with their teenagers. The ideal goal is to achieve a close, warm, mutually loving relationship. However, the fact is that some parents and children do not particularly like one another because of family differences or difficulties that have not yet been resolved.

Factors which place stress upon a relationship are both intrapersonal (occurring within the person) and interpersonal (motivated from external objects or people). Intrapersonal factors include developmental changes associated with teenage and mid-life transitions, the individual personalities of child and parent, any distortions of perception caused by drug or alcohol abuse, and the perception of roles as learned through family communication. Interpersonal factors include such areas as the teen's respect for authority. This lesson is taught by parents, but it is also taught by extended family members, community schools, religious institutions, and through peer interaction. For example, over the last forty years the power held by authority figures has lessened to the point that teens rebel at decisions that would not have been questioned by earlier generations.

During the teen years, parents are often "held hostage" when their teen complains that "all my friends do it." How can you as a parent forcibly keep your child from peers you consider less than desirable? As a parent, the one fact you must face is that you cannot "keep" your child away from certain people. You can yell or quietly state your concerns about a particular friend. But unless you follow your child twenty-four hours a day, the child can choose to be with that person. The point here is that you must accept the limits of your power over the teen. You might best keep your child away by stating your concerns. If the child says you aren't being fair since you don't know this particular person, you need to ask yourself that question. If you have been too quick to judge, then admit your mistake. Is it not better to admit your error than to rely on the rigid approach—"I'm your parent and you have to listen to me"? This only tends to send the teen closer to the person who might truly prove a poor influence.

Me-generation parents too often allow their teens to interact with all types of people. They may ignore early signs of problems. If your teen suddenly begins to test curfews, lose interest and pride in school grades, or appear drunk or drugged, don't ignore this behavior. At the same time, don't overreact. Should you "ignore" the situation when your child admits having used drugs, says "I have stopped," but refuses to give up the scale (used to weigh drugs) and papers (used to roll marijuana cigarettes)? How can parents overlook their child's need for supervision? How has the world changed, and how do today's teens develop values often vastly different from those of their parents?

For some parents, childhood memories recall the fanciful and idealized parents from "Leave It to Beaver" and "Father Knows Best." Television presents each generation with a different picture and message about parents and families. There's a drastic difference in contemporary television models as compared to those shown to parents as they were growing up. For example, there is a great allure and an idealistic presentation in the models found in such shows as "Little House on the Prairie" and "The Waltons." However, the young who watch the full range of examples available will find a countereffect in "Soap" and "Three's Company." (It is important to know that these shows often appear as reruns.)

When children watch "Three's Company," they see a young single man who lives with two women, gets into "problems," and solves them each week in a thirty-minute segment. Information obtained in clinical practice revealed that many families see the viewing of such shows as a harmless free-time activity. However, when the content of the program was described as a situation in which a neighbor might be engaged, the parents were certain they would shield their child from such an influence. They failed to see that, in a sense, they were approving this type of behavior by not blocking its message to their child.

The point is that today's parent is attempting to raise a child who may hold a different view of the world. It is critical to note who and what influence the teen.

Intrapersonal Issues Affecting the Adult

In *Human Development and Education*, R. Havighurst describes the major developmental tasks that create the intrapersonal agenda on which parents consciously or unconsciously build a relationship. Havighurst (see table) specifies periods of early adulthood (18-35), middle age (35-60), and later maturity (60 and over).

Specific tasks associated with each stage can serve as major supports for the relationship with the teen, or they can provide fuel for the fire in the struggle between parent and child. For example, most parents of teens are in or entering the "middle age" experience. (Some authors call this mid-life crisis.)

The early adulthood and middle-age tasks are part

ADULT DEVELOPMENTAL TASKS

Early Adulthood (18-35)

- Select a mate.
- Learn to live with a marriage partner.
- Start a family.
- Rear children.
- Manage a home.
- Get started in an occupation.
- Take on civic responsibility.
- Find a congenial social group.

Middle Age (35-60)

- Achieve Adult civic and social responsibility.
- Establish and maintain an economic standard of living.
- Assist teenage children to become responsible and happy adults.
- Develop adult leisure-time activities.
- Relate oneself to one's spouse as a person.
- Accept and adjust to the physiological changes of middle age.
- Adjust to aging parents.

Later Maturity (60 and over)

- Adjust to decreasing physical strength and health.
- Adjust to retirement and reduced income.
- Adjust to death of spouse.
- Establish an explicit affiliation with one's age group.
- Meet social and civic obligations.
- Establish satisfactory physical living arrangements.

---

of many family systems. Not all people engage these tasks in a stressful, anxious fashion. Nonetheless, as you look over the specific tasks associated with the age periods, you can see that lack of resolution of any or all of them would affect the way you currently see and deal with your teen.

Let us examine the situation of a forty-two-year-old steel worker, the father of a teenage son. Because of layoffs in the steel industry, the father faced a sizable cut in pay and possible loss of his job. Although his wife was employed and there was some money to count on, it was no wonder the father was short-tempered.

Arguments with the son were sparked when the teenager failed to come home on time. The parents also complained that he wore his hair too long, listened to hard rock, drank beer on weekends, and was "lazy." His grades were passing, but he was not "working up to his potential."

The parents initially were unable to see that the family's economic instability was to some extent responsible for their son's "uncooperative and rebellious" behavior. And in a sense, the son was "breaking away"—confused about asserting his independence and testing the limits of parental authority. The father, whose sense of self-worth and security were affected by the uncertainty of employment, was unconsciously seeking to retain control of his son.

How could this or any relationship be maintained and improved? All relationships take work. If a period of poor communication has taken place, what can a parent do to improve relations? The answer lies in how parent and teen assess the situation and what they decide to do to bring about change.

Intelligence

How can parents help to develop their teenager's intelligence? Few people know how smart they really are. The IQ, or intelligence quotient score measures only part of one's intelligence. For example, IQ scores show how much verbal, mathematical, memory, and spatial ability a person has. They measure skills related to school or career success. But psychologists have named at least thirty-seven factors necessary for estimating human intelligence. In fact, one psychologist cites one hundred twenty ways the mind interprets the world.

In a recent book, *Frames of Mind: The Theory of Multiple Intelligence,* Howard Gardener describes six areas of intelligence—linguistic, musical, logical-mathematical, spatial, bodily-kinesthetic, and personal. These areas tell much more about a person's ability than can be learned from a single IQ score. Gardener divides these intelligences into separate areas, since each has its own set of operations, or procedures, and biological basis.

Linguistic intelligence is defined as the ability to use and understand the meaning and communication of language and rules of grammar; this includes sensitivity to sounds, rhythms, and meters of words. Musical intelligence explores an individual's appreciation of music and ability to create musical compositions. The logical-mathematical domain measures a person's proficiency with logical properties of thought, objects, and numbers. Spatial intelligence refers to the ability to think and imagine visually. Bodily-kinesthetic intelligence describes the level of physical ability. Last, personal intelligence refers to the ability to notice the characteristics of other individuals—in particular, their moods, temperaments, motivations, and intentions.

A highly developed sense of personal intelligence can be seen in such leaders as Mahatma Gandhi and Martin Luther King—and also in skilled parents, teachers, and therapists. Personal intelligence is the ability to assess a person's feelings about life (that is, the full range of emotions), discriminate among those feelings, and eventually name and use them to understand and guide behavior.

Parents teach their child about personal intelligence by the way they value that child's education. A daughter of one couple was the third oldest of six children. She was forced to quit school in the tenth grade because she was "needed" to care for the younger children. Only one of the younger sisters eventually completed high school, in spite of the fact that all the children were of average to above-average intelligence.

The daughter grew up feeling she was "dumb" because she had not finished high school. She blamed herself, although the parents had controlled the decision not to continue in school. The daughter married, eventually obtained a high school equivalency degree, and enrolled in a college two-year associate degree program. It took therapy, tutors, and the urging of her two grown children and husband, but she finally made it!

This woman's doubts were not easily overcome, since the idea that she was too "dumb" to go to school was taught by her parents when she was young. The result shows that as her personal intelligence grew and she dealt with her feelings, she was able to understand why her parents had made her quit school, and she eventually chose to continue her education.

In another example, a fifteen-year-old only child learned to achieve at a high level, but failed to develop in other important areas. His school work varied from excellent to fair, although tests showed that his verbal and mathematical abilities and eye-hand coordination were very superior and that he could use these skills. Emotional testing, however, showed that the child was low in self-confidence, nervous, and unhappy.

The parents, both successful professionals, were counseled to encourage their child's social and emotional development and ease off on the importance of high grades. These high-achievement parents were advised to minimize the pressure on their child in order to maximize his growth in other areas of development.

Psychologists argue that intelligence is an inherited trait, but that environment can either nurture or limit the use of this potential. Some people with seemingly high intelligence fail to show it in their lives. What conditions limit their success?

Educational opportunities and economic or social conditions are environmental factors that affect the individual. The key to successful development of both teen and parent is the growth of personal intelligence. Ultimately, a diminished personal intelligence can limit the way you and your teen use the potential in the other areas of intelligence.

Video Music

How do parents deal with the effects of this medium on their teenagers?

If you were told there's a revolution on television that has whisked away children like a modern Pied Piper, would you guess the recent appearance of video music programs as the cause?

These programs have changed the way the music industry markets the Top 40 on both cable and noncable channels. Since the video music format presents songs with pictures, the "new music" market has swooped down to capture preschoolers, along with the preteen and teenage audience.

Preschoolers are hooked because pictures hold their attention. Videos are short and catchy, cartoon-like in length and, some professionals believe, in the way they distort reality. The music includes Top 40, rock, hard rock, and country, so most tastes can be accommodated. Formats vary from a singer or a group in concert to a short story directly related to the lyrics, to a collection of unrelated visuals which show symbolically sexual and violent themes.

Video rock is daily television consumption for millions of children. They watch before and after school. They dance, sing, and learn from their video heroes. As a result, schoolteachers supervise break-dance contests and principals need to decide whether white spangled gloves violate school dress codes.

Psychologists and guidance counselors are expressing concern over videos that model sexual and violent themes. For example, in one musical story, you might see a rejected lover break the old love's picture, strike people, or smash guitars. The message tells children that anger and frustration may be vented in an antisocial way.

In another story, the portrayal of young love has taken a new twist with a combination of sex and violence. In this country video, the action takes place in a bar. The lyrics tell of conflict between two females over a man. A man and woman find each other across the smoke-filled room. The female walks over and begins to kiss the man. Enter the "old" girlfriend, who tries to separate the two. The females engage in a symbolic fight, while the man watches, emotionless. In the last scene, the new woman and the man fall into an embrace on a couch.

What does this teach? The liberated-female theme has taken on a new message in which love is distorted by lust.The values of the bar are played out in a story which rewards people who act out of lust. The image of love is based solely on sex, which initially attracted the lovers.

Potential negative effects of these videos may not

be visible immediately, but will appear over the years. In summertime, the children who watch video music leave school and hit the streets, leaving psychologists and guidance counselors to ponder the fallout. They report that video music has had more negative effect than merely the often-observed interest in break dancing, music magazines, and the occasional hands painted white.

School officials are bewildered by the heavy music video viewers, who appear apathetic. These children develop an I-don't-care-about-anything-except-video-music attitude. They seem to drop out. Their parents report that they no longer participate in previously enjoyed activities. They forget sports, friends, and family mealtimes. They use video music to meet social needs; it gives them experiences to share with friends, and may be the only friend of some.

One fourteen-year-old girl, overweight and an acne victim, the youngest of three and the only one at home, had a history of poor peer relationships and also often talked back to teachers who disciplined her misbehavior. She was not involved in after-school activities but remained in her room to watch music video. Her parents did not regulate television watching since she always had been a low-average student. They failed to notice that televised music was becoming so important.

This teenager used video music to find friends; she watched it to have something to talk about, and even brought music magazines to share with her school "friends." Perhaps it was because of her emotional outbursts with teachers or her lack of social maturity, but she was not accepted by her peers. In response, she remained a heavy and unhappy viewer without normal social outlets. This child was isolated and at risk, using video music as an escape.

In some cases, such a constant viewing habit is a way to get parental attention, even though the attention is negative. Since parents are usually not interested in the music or the performers, the child can use it to create parent-child conflict. For example, one teenage boy watched videos day and night. Fascination with rock magazines and heroes replaced his interest in sports and friends. In his search to "look like the stars," the boy donned an earring and let his hair grow.

His parents fought with him over the length of his hair but didn't realize that the earring was worn at school and on dates. The child was asserting himself to find his identity. But his parents grew tired of his constant conversation about music and turned him off until he failed two subjects at school. Then they decided to monitor and limit his music involvement and talk with him about his interests and his school performance.

On the other hand, parents who support a child's interest in music videos can also foster poor school performance. These parents see it as a harmless activity. One child who was a heavy video viewer loved music. His parents nurtured his interest with records, magazines, drum and piano lessons. But his teacher observed that as the boy's interest in music grew, his grades dropped; he handed in incomplete work and often stared into space. When the parents followed the psychologist's recommendation that video viewing be limited, the child's school performance improved and other interests besides music developed.

School officials would be wise to devise ways to channel young people's interest in music into educational methods. In a Philadelphia school's pilot project, junior high students who are low-ability readers have learned skills by reading rules as lyrics. This new technique has worked where traditional methods failed.

Although most children are not addicted to video music programs, even light viewers will see one of the messages that video sells—the use of violence to handle angry feelings. They meet their friends and relate to the buzz of a box as they hang out at malls, corners, and schoolyards.

How will parents cope with the oft-repeated pleas of children—What can I do now? Will the modern parent say, "Why don't you break dance, honey?" or just, "Beat it!"?

Parents and Peers

Teenagers spend more time with their friends than with their parents because they have more in common. Parents undergo a loss of the closeness they may have shared with their teens when they were younger. This loss is often expressed by finding fault with the teens, arguing over behaviors that previously would have been overlooked. Parents might also say they don't like their teens' new friends, when in fact there might not be anything wrong or out of the ordinary with them. At this point, it is crucial for parents to do some reflective thinking and attempt to maturely look at and live with this new evolving relationship with their teens, who are growing up and eventually will leave home.

It is a fact that most children grow up and live their own lives. You may consciously know that your child will grow and leave you, but you may not be aware of your unconscious or "hidden" needs. For example, is your child like a close friend, sharing perhaps too much knowledge concerning problems in your marriage? Is your teen the person who will be and do all the things you never could (go to college or marry a rich partner)? How do you really perceive the role of the teen in the family?

On the other hand, does your teen "need" you to make a decision? This need could be as basic as allowing you to pick out clothing, or more complex, such as the question of the real values in life. Perhaps the greatest cause of concern becomes evident when teens begin to date in a serious fashion. If and when a teen falls in love, parents are aware there is a great probability that, somewhere down the road, the relationship might end. Some parents who desire to protect their teen from an experience that could result in an emotional loss become overly involved.

Others are greatly concerned that their teen will not resist the sexual advances of opposite-sex friends. What is the happy medium in such a situation?

There are a number of questions to consider as your teen enters the world of dating:

1. *Is your child clear as to your position and feeling about relationships with the opposite sex?* This applies not only to mastery of sexual involvement, but to other areas: Who are the people your teen wants to go out with? Will the date be as a couple or within a group situation? How will transportation be handled—will a parent be driving or will a competent teen be behind the wheel? How often will an older teen be allowed to use a family car? What about curfew times? Should you meet potential friends before the teen can go on a date? These are reasonable questions.

2. *Have you as a parent adequately educated your teen as to the functioning of his or her body?* Does your child know how fertilization takes place? Are you comfortable with the emergence of your child's sexual feelings? Are you fright-end? Are you jealous?

3. *How will you assess your child's emotional and/or sexual involvement with dates?* Will you attempt a third-degree approach when your teen enters the door after a date? How can you ask your teen about relationships or feelings if you have not developed communication over

less explosive matters during the teen's younger years? Whatever you attempt, do not subscribe to the philosophy "out of sight, out of mind," or "If I don't see a problem I won't be concerned."

If you have taught your child your values concerning love and marriage, you have provided a sound foundation upon which your teen will base a choice. Yes, the teen has the power. Because unless you are with your child twenty-four hours a day, he or she has the freedom of choice. Parents live with the reality that their teenager might become involved in sexual behaviors of which they disagree or disapprove. You do not want to create a great distance between yourself and your teen so that there is fear of coming to you if a problem arises—for instance, an unplanned pregnancy. You need not keep the idea in mind that your teen will become pregnant, but at the same time, you don't want to create such great fear or shame that your child would stay away in time of need. What are families for, and how strong and close is your family, if your teen could not come to you in a time of crisis? These questions apply not only to dating and friends, but to all areas of your relationship.

Parents can and should teach wholesome values. They should model these behaviors and talk about how a man and a woman can build a solid relationship. But there is no formula. It might be best to say that parents need to teach their teen to live independently in the world. In short, it seems that the role of parenthood is to work oneself out of a "job" and into a relationship with an adult who will leave home to build his or her own life.

Critical Steps in Improving the Relationship Between Parent and Teen

1. *Assess the type of relationship that currently exists,* then improve the weaker points by maximizing the strengths.

2. *Accept the possibility that you may grieve over the loss of the closeness* experienced when your child was younger. For example, a mother might regret that her son, who used to share so openly the events in his day, now acts close-mouthed about what happened at school, at a dance, or with his friends. This pulling away is an attempt, in many cases, to assert identity and independence. If the mother can understand why she "needs" her child, she can learn to interact in a manner free of conflict.

3. *Teenagers may talk about behaviors and values contrary to the ones by which you were raised* or in which you believe, so that they can test what they truly value and, by doing so, exert their sense of identity. In order to decide whether you should be upset or angry when your teen expresses an opinion, you should look beyond the words and examine the actions. For example, if you and your teen argue over the merits of capitalism versus communism,

should you panic *before* your adolescent actually joins the Communist Party or goes to political rallies, or do you panic at the mere mention of inequalities in the capitalistic system? It may be most difficult to maintain an objective stance in response to this diverse political ideology. However, you might best serve the relationship by interacting with your child as if you were two people on a television show such as "Face the Nation," and not fight World War Three!

4. *Try to serve as a consultant to most of your teenagers' decisions.* Since you want your child to learn independence, express your opinions and feelings when your teen strives to do and say things free of your decisions, and at times of your feelings. Don't expect to be accepted and treated objectively. Since the give and take of discussion and debate may be new, your teen may not be as able as you to handle the one-on-one of these verbal exchanges. Therefore you as the adult will need to assume the roles of both participant and referee in order to minimize aggressive language and behavior. If you fail to achieve a sense of calm or composure, the heat of the moment may result in an adversarial style of relating. In order to improve relationships in your home, think of ways your daily activities can bridge differences and distance within the parent-child relationship.

5. *Clearly define the behavior you expect from your teen,* especially if you have strong feelings about certain areas. For example, if your teen abuses alcohol or drugs, you can be firm in stating that these substances are not permitted in the home. You will be better "heard," of course, if you yourself limit your own alcohol or drug use. Doing otherwise only demonstrates a rather hypocritical stance on your part.

CHAPTER 6

Evaluating the Teen/Parent Relationship: Working for Quality Time

Parent and teen often desire a positive relationship but have difficulty attaining it. This chapter contains a series of questions to examine how each of you sees the relationship and what each can do to improve your family life. Whether you live in an intact, single-parent, or blended family, or just want to get closer to a teenager, the following surveys will help clarify ways you and your teen can work together and relate more effectively. The forms should be completed on separate sheets of paper, by both parent and teen where appropriate, and used as a point of discussion afterward. (Actually, forms 1, 2, and 3 should have been completed before reading this book.) Included are forms for:

Adult and Teen Relationship Histories
Identification of Time Together
Family Interaction
Positive and Negative Reactions
Goals and Contract
Activity Assessment.

The Relationship History forms should be filled out first, to give both teen and adult a starting point concerning the nature of the relationship. The Time Together form allows family members an opportunity to determine just how much activity time they want to spend together. The teen and adult Family Interaction surveys further heighten awareness of interaction within the relationship, as do the Positive and Negative Reactions sheets. Finally, if desired, the Contract form can be used as a way to agree on the direction both parent and teen wish the relationship to take. If further evaluation of family time is required after changes or goals have been agreed upon, the Activity Assessment form would be useful in determining the strengths and weaknesses in family relationships.

ADULT:
HISTORY OF RELATIONSHIP

NAME:

1. How long have you had a relationship with the teenager(s) in your life?

   Length of time:________ years ________ months

2. How would you describe this relationship? Place a check mark in the appropriate space below:

   ____ overall satisfying

   ____ mostly satisfying

   ____ somewhat satisfying

   ____ not satisfying

3. How often was your relationship with the teen(s) mutually satisfying? Place a check mark:

   ______ generally ______ seldom ______ never

   Cite examples: *Age of teen(s) at that time:*

   1. ______________ ______________________

   2. ______________ ______________________

   3. ______________ ______________________

4. What was the nature of the time spent with the teen(s)?

   ____ a. We mostly talked together.

   ____ b. We mostly played board games.

____ c. We mostly played outside sports and activities.

____ d. We enjoyed experiences without other people present.

____ e. Other (please describe) ____________

____

____

____

____

5. Based on the examples you gave in Question 3, place a check mark beside the appropriate situations.

____ a. We could talk easily.

____ b. I was able to give information.

____ c. We both enjoyed the activity.

____ d. When the teen was younger, I was able to teach skills during an activity.

____ e. We both laughed during the activity or talked later about how we enjoyed it.

____ f. I was able to tell the teen how well he/she did the activity.

____ g. Other (please describe) ____________

____

____

____

____

Turn to the Relationship History Evaluation on page 127. Read and answer the questions for each of the above items you checked. After completing your answers, review them with the teen answers.

TEEN:
HISTORY OF RELATIONSHIP

NAME:

1. How long have you had a relationship with the significant adult(s) in your life? (parents, step-parents, or friend of a parent).

Name: *Length of time: Years Months*

1. ____________________ __________ _______

2. ____________________ __________ _______

2. How would you describe this relationship? Place a check mark in the appropriate space below:

 ___ overall satisfying

 ___ mostly satisfying

 ___ somewhat satisfying

 ___ not satisfying

3. How often was your relationship with the adult(s) mutually satisfying? Place a check mark:

 ___ generally ___ seldom ___ never

 Cite examples: *Your age at that time:*

 1. ______________ ________________________

 2. ______________ ________________________

 3. ______________ ________________________

4. What was the nature of the time spent with the adult(s)?

    ____ a. We mostly talked together.

    ____ b. We mostly played board games.

    ____ c. We mostly played outside sports and activities.

    ____ d. We enjoyed experiences without other people present.

    ____ e. Other (please describe) ________________

    ____

    ____

    ____

5. Based on the examples you gave in Question 3, place a check mark beside the appropriate situations.

    ____ a. We could talk easily.

    ____ b. I was able to give information.

    ____ c. We both enjoyed the activity.

    ____ d. When I was younger, he/she taught me how to do things.

    ____ e. We laughed when doing things or talked about them later.

    ____ f. He/she told me how well I was doing an activity. ("You throw a mean curve ball" or "You're a good chess player.")

___ g. Other (please describe) ______________________

____

____

____

____

Turn to the Relationship History Evaluation on page 127. Read and answer the questions for each of the above items you checked. After completing your answers, review them with the adult answers.

ADULT AND TEEN: RELATIONSHIP HISTORY EVALUATION QUESTIONS

(answer on a separate sheet)

For each item you checked in Question 5 of the Adult or Teen form, answer the following questions.

a. Communication

The ability to communicate is basic to enjoying any activity. Do you have this skill?

____ Most times.

____ I should improve this.

What will I need to do to improve my ability to communicate?

____

____

In what ways have you changed communication habits to limit or improve activities?

Changes That Limit Good Communication	Changes That Have Improved Communication
1.	1.
2.	2.
3.	3.

b. *Giving Information*

When the teen was younger, did either of you teach the other an activity?	___Yes	___No
During those times, could each of you teach the other in a noncritical way?	___Yes	___No
Have you noted an increase in arguments when the adult tries to inform during the teenage years?	___Yes	___No
Does the adult listen when the teen explains things?	___Yes	___No

c. *Enjoyment of Activities*

Did you enjoy activities together when the teen was younger (13-15)?	___Yes	___No
Was there discussion of those pleasant times?	___Yes	___No
Do you still enjoy the activities, together or alone?	___Yes	___No
Can you currently talk about enjoyable times?	___Yes	___No

d. Teaching Skills

Did the teen ever teach the adult skills for a hobby or sport? ___Yes ___No

List Skills Taught	*Age of Teen at That Time*
1. ____________	____________
2. ____________	____________
3. ____________	____________

Does the teen currently do the activity? ___Yes ___No

Has the adult taught the teen skills during the teen years? ___Yes ___No

List Skills Taught	*Age of Teen at That Time*
1. ____________	____________
2. ____________	____________
3. ____________	____________

How have you enhanced or limited the effective teaching experiences?

Ways I have Enhanced the Other's Teaching	*Ways I Have Rejected the Other's Teaching*
1.	1.
2.	2.
3.	3.

e. Talking About Good Times

Were either or both of you able to talk with each other about experiences together? ___Yes ___No

Were you able to talk about these times with other family members? ___Yes ___No

Did the teen ever initiate these positive dialogues? ___Yes ___No

Cite an example:______________________________

____

Did the teen freely engage in these positive dialogues? ___Yes ___No

Cite an example:______________________________

____

How would you describe current dialogue?______

____

f. Positive Praise Factor

Was the adult able to praise the teen for performance during an activity? ("You really know how to play chess.") ___Yes ___No

Cite an example:____________________________

____

For Adults:

Were you able to talk about the performance of the teen with friends? ___Yes ___No

For Teens:

Do you currently receive praise directly from the adult? ___Yes ___No

Cite examples:____________________________

____

____

Is praise about the teen currently given to friends or relatives and learned of indirectly by the teen? ___Yes ___No

Cite examples:____________________________

____

____

ADULT AND TEEN: DESCRIPTION OF THE RELATIONSHIP

(answer on a separate sheet)

Nature of Activity

For Adults:

Were you interested in action-oriented activities? ___Yes ___No

Were you interested in quiet or sitting-type activities? ___Yes ___No

For Teens:

Were you interested in action-oriented activities? ___Yes ___No

Were you interested in quiet or sitting-type activities? ___Yes ___No

For Both:

What kinds of activities do the two of you currently engage in?

Cite examples:____________________________

____

Time Alone with the Teen

Were teen and adult able to spend enjoyable times alone together? ___Yes ___No

Example:_________________________________

____

____

Are the teen and adult currently able to spend enjoyable time together? ___Yes ___No

Example:___________________________________

Do other family members join the current enjoyable times? ___Yes ___No

Example:___________________________________

Did the teen show any difference in behavior when alone with adult, as compared to times with other family members? ___Yes ___No

Example:___________________________________

Current Activities

How much time do you currently spend doing things together? Hours per Week:______

Describe recent positive and negative times together:

Positive	*Negative*
____________	____________
____________	____________
____________	____________
____________	____________
____________	____________
____________	____________

ADULT AND TEEN: IDENTIFICATION OF TIMES TO SPEND TOGETHER

(answer on a separate sheet)

NAME:

1. At what times would it be possible for you to be together?

	Each Weekday	*Saturday*	*Sunday*
Hours	____	____	____
Minutes	____	____	____

2. The best times to spend together are:

   1.

   2.

3. List each family member. Place a check under the heading that best describes how you spend time with that person:

Family Member	Average of Time Spent	Mostly Work	Mostly Play	Combined Work & Play
a.				
b.				
c.				
d.				
e.				
f.				

Who do you do chores with most? ____________

Who do you play with most? ____________

Who do you spend little time with? ____________

Who do you spend most time with? ____________

ADULT:
FAMILY INTERACTION

Place a check beside each statement that tends to describe you or how you feel about your family.

_____ 1. I am able to help my teen by talking about issues of concern to young people.

_____ 2. I am often in conflict with my teen.

_____ 3. I am concerned about the daily activities of my teen.

_____ 4. I find myself so involved in other responsibilities, I'm often too busy for my teen.

_____ 5. I am able to talk to my teen about behavior without becoming so emotional or angry that the issue is never resolved.

_____ 6. Although I know I should feel positive toward my teen, I cannot.

_____ 7. I am unable to see my teen as an individual.

_____ 8. I feel it easier to relate to people outside the family than to my own children.

_____ 9. I am able to show a real interest in the life of my teen (watch sport events, discuss topics of interest).

_____10. I am often critical of my teen.

_____11. I am willing to do most things my teen asks even if he (she) is able to do it alone.

______12. I do not feel close to my teen.

______13. I am able to show affection toward the teen in our family by hugging or saying how much I care.

______14. I often monitor the use of time since my teen seems not to be acting appropriately.

______15. I don't let my teen make her (his) own share of mistakes.

______16. I have difficulty participating in activities with my teen.

______17. I am able to be a responsible parent in the direction and guidance I give regarding such issues as job choice or the handling of difficult situations.

______18. As the parent, I almost always know best, but my teen seems to challenge me.

______19. I want to take part in activities with my teen and often say that he (she) is too involved with other people or activities.

______20. I do not feel we are a close-knit family, since each of us is too busy doing his or her own thing.

TEEN: FAMILY INTERACTION

_____ 1. I am willing and able to help my parent(s) with household responsibilities.

_____ 2. I struggle with my parent(s) over the things I want to do, but they seem not to understand.

_____ 3. I help my parent(s) any time, even if I have to change my own plans.

_____ 4. I want to spend more time with my friends than with my parent(s).

_____ 5. I am able to openly tell my parent(s) what is on my mind without losing my "cool" and telling them off.

_____ 6. I feel angry about the way this family fights over little things.

_____ 7. I prefer to be with my parent(s) rather than with friends.

_____ 8. My parent(s) don't seem to care that I am not involved with things at home.

_____ 9. I show an interest in the life of my parent(s) by listening to topics they wish to discuss, or by listening to their criticism of me.

_____10. I am not willing to assume responsibilities in this family since my parent(s) are supposed to do those things.

_____11. I am not allowed to do as many things as other teens my age.

______12. I feel my life is more important than my parents think it is.

______13. I feel positive toward my parent(s) because they have done a good job of teaching me to live on my own.

______14. I cannot openly tell my parent(s) what I am thinking without losing my temper or feeling resentful.

______15. I feel responsible for important household jobs.

______16. When I am close to my parents, I begin to feel uncomfortable.

______17. I feel a closeness toward my parent(s) and could discuss many private issues like dating, career choices, and angry feelings.

______18. I do not feel positive toward one (or both) parent(s).

______19. I am concerned about what one member of my family is doing that saddens the rest of us.

______20. I feel I am not aware of my parent(s) concerns for the family or feelings about life.

ADULT AND TEEN: FAMILY INTERACTION EVALUATION

If you checked most of Questions 1, 5, 9, 13, and 17, your family appears more *cooperative,* and the following statements might describe it.

1. Family members are able to work together.
2. Family members are able to solve problems.
3. Adult(s) and teen(s) have their needs met.
4. Communication is open and comfortable.
5. Adult(s) and teen(s) show interest in one another's activities.
6. Adult(s) and teen(s) show positive regard for one another.
7. Adult(s) and teen(s) feel close to one another.

If you checked most of Questions 2, 6, 10, 14, and 18, your family appears more *adversarial,* and the following statements might describe it:

1. There are power struggles between adult(s) and teen(s).
2. There seems to be an inability to resolve conflict.
3. There is a lack of open communication.
4. There are unclear rules and expectations.
5. Boundary issues are unclear.
6. There is little positive regard between adult(s) and teen(s).
7. Family members feel constrained, lack autonomy, and fight for control.

If you checked most of Questions 3, 7, 11, 15, and 19, your family appears to have *overinvolved* parent(s), and the following statements might describe it.

1. Parent(s) in this family are truly concerned, but block teen(s) from a reasonable amount of peer involvement and appropriate emotional development.
2. Parents' expectations of teen(s) are not based on the level of teen(s) abilities.
3. Parent(s) express opinions about the overall functioning of family members but see only their perception for family happiness, ignoring the teen(s). For example, one member of the family may present a problem such as poor grades, or alcohol abuse, but the family might not work to end the problem. Rather, teens may be expected to carry out adult responsibilities.

If you checked most of Questions 4, 8, 12, 16, and 20, your family appears more *underinvolved,* and the following statements might describe it.

1. Teen(s) and adult(s) are preoccupied with self-interests. There may be a high degree of role reversal, with the teen(s) assuming many household responsibilities.
2. The uninvolved state of a parent and/or teen creates undue conflict for teen(s) since little intimacy is established.
3. There can be open hostility when either parent(s) or teen(s) feel burdened by the other.
4. Holidays and birthdays are not enjoyable times together.

ADULT AND TEEN: POSITIVE AND NEGATIVE REACTIONS

(answer on a separate sheet)

All families have disagreements. Problems can occur infrequently or on a regular basis. Please respond to the following questions:

Cite one problem that occurs *infrequently* (example: teen receives an F on a test).

1.

Cite positive reaction.

Cite negative reaction.

Cite one problem that occurs *frequently* (example: parent abuses alcohol).

1.

Cite positive reaction.

Cite negative reaction.

For both the infrequent and the frequent (chronic) situation(s), respond to the following questions with I for infrequent or C for chronic.

Positive Reaction	*Negative Reaction*
1. a.____ All the people involved were able to express thoughts about solving the problem.	b.____ Few people in the discussion expressed thoughts about solving the problem.
2. a.____ People were able to argue without hurting peoples' feelings.	b.____ People said hurtful things to one another.

3. a.____ No unrelated or past problems were brought up.
   b._____ Other unrelated or past problems were brought up.
4. a.____ If people took sides, the solution to the problem didn't leave anyone with a feeling of "us" against "them."
   b._____ I felt they won and I lost (or I won and they lost).
5. a.____ I don't feel anyone (parent or teen) controlled words or actions.
   b._____ I felt someone (parent or teen) controlled words or actions.
6. a.____ People listened without interrupting while others spoke.
   b._____ People interrupted one another.
7. a.____ People responded completely to concerns or questions raised by others.
   b._____ People didn't answer concerns or questions raised.
8. a.____ Those who were upset said things that showed they understood others.
   b._____ People in the discussion didn't understand or listen to others.
9. a.____ No one threatened to use physical force and no one broke anything.
   b._____ Threats of force or destruction of property occurred.

10. a.____ If punishment was given, it fit the misbehavior.

b.____ If punishment was given, it was too stiff.

Cite goals you need to set for your behavior in order to create more cooperative dialogue for both the infrequent and the chronic situation.

Infrequent Goal	*Chronic Goal*
1.	
2.	
3.	
4.	

TEEN AND ADULT: GOAL CONTRACT

Based upon the completion of the forms in this section, cite goals both parent and teen find important for improving the situation in your family. On a separate sheet, create a form similar to the following:

I, ______________________________, promise to

____

____

____

when an argument or misunderstanding occurs in our home.

____

(sign here)

____

(date)

TEEN AND ADULT: ACTIVITY ASSESSMENT

(answer on a separate sheet)

After allowing some time to pass, answer the following questions to assess your attempts to create a more cooperative family environment.

1. Have you spent more time interacting in enjoyable activities?

   Yes_____ No_____

   Cite examples:

   1.

   2.

2. Have you made concrete changes to reach specific goals?

   Yes_____ No_____

   Cite examples:

   1.

   2.

3. Does each feel understood by the other?

   _____ improved

   _____ about the same

   _____ less understood

4. Do you feel professional help is needed to improve family interaction?

   a._____Yes _____No

b. What kind of help? Check as many as you like:

_____ Clergy

_____ Mental Health

_____ Medical

_____ School Counselor

_____ Other:_______________________________

5. Does your family meet in order to talk about issues and to spend enjoyable times together?

_____Yes _____No

6. Cite specific strengths developed by both parent and teen.

	Adult(s)	Teen
a.		
b.		

7. Cite areas still needing improvement:

	Adult(s)	Teen
a.		
b.		

EPILOGUE

When there is effort on the part of families, there is hope for improved relationships between family members. Having listened to the concerns of parents and teenagers alike, the authors realize the necessity for a book on this area of family life. In effect, this book begins where *Real Men Enjoy Their Kids* ends. All ages and periods of development appear to be fraught with conflict; family interaction, especially adolescent/parent involvement, seems typically difficult. We hope this text will show families that there can be resolution of both the routine and the not-so-routine problems.

Most families with teenagers will profit from the material contained here. For the greatest benefit, the issues raised might well be discussed by teen and parent together. It seems critical that all family members understand the impact each inevitably has on the others. Although the ideas and concepts in this volume at times appear self-evident, they are continually overlooked or regarded as superfluous. In our opinion, they are the ingredients of meaningful interaction and quality time.

Professional helpers—counselors, social workers, psychologists, psychiatrists, clergy—may find this book useful in their work. Ultimately, the material could enhance their already existing thoughts on teen/parent relations.

With well-intentioned hard work, the ideas contained in this text will sharpen the skills necessary for developing the quality moments that allow for individual and collective family growth. For all of us with teens or teens-to-be, we wish time well spent in developing the best possible moments together.

BIBLIOGRAPHY

Bell, Ruth, and Zeiger, Levi. *Talking with Your Teenager: A Book for Parents.* New York: Random House, 1983.

Cohen, Rebecca S.; Cohler, Bertram J.; and Weissman, Sidney H., eds. *Parenthood: A Psychodynamic Perspective.* New York: Guilford Press, 1984.

Davitz, Lois, and Davitz, Joel. *How to Live (Almost) Happily with a Teenager.* New York: New American Library, 1982.

Elkind, David. *All Grown Up and No Place to Go: Teenagers in Crisis.* Reading, Mass.: Addison Wesley Publishing Co., 1984.

Ephron, D. *Teenage Romance.* New York: Ballantine Books, 1981.

Francke, Linda B. *Growing Up Divorced.* New York: Fawcett Books, 1984.

Gardner, Howard. *Frames of Mind: The Theory of Multiple Intelligences.* New York: Basic Books, 1983.

Giffin, Mary, and Felsenthal, Carol. *A Cry for Help: Exploring and Exploding the Myths About Teenage Suicide.* New York: Doubleday, 1983.

Glenbard East Echo, comp. *Teenagers Themselves.* New York: Adama Publications, 1984.

Gross, L. H., ed. *The Parents' Guide to Teenagers.* New York: Macmillan, 1981.

Kaplan, Louise J. *Adolescence: A Farewell to Childhood.* New York: Simon & Schuster, 1984.

Levinson, Daniel J.; Darrow, Charlotte N.; Klein, Edward B.; Levinson, Maria H.; and McKee, Braxton. *The Seasons of a Man's Life.* New York: Alfred A. Knopf, 1978; Ballantine Books, 1979.

McCoy, K. *Coping with Teenage Depression.* New York: New American Library, 1982.

Norman, J., and Harris, M. *The Private Life of the American Teenager.* New York: Rawson-Wade, 1981.

Offer, Daniel, and Sabshin, Melvin, eds. *Normality Through the Life Cycle: A Critical Integration.* New York: Basic Books, 1984.

Schaefer, Charles E.; Briesmeister, James M.; and Fitten, Maureen E., eds. *Family Therapy Techniques for Problem Behaviors of Children and Teenagers.* San Francisco: Jossey-Bass, 1984.

Shechtman, Stephen A. "IQ Is Only Part of the Story," *The Sunday Globe Times*, Bethlehem, Penna. (August 19, 1984).

Shechtman, Stephen A. "What Is TV Teaching Your Kids?" *The Sunday Globe Times*, Bethlehem, Penna. (February 12, 1984).

Shechtman, Stephen A. "What Ever Happened to Innocence of Childhood?" *The Sunday Globe Times*, Bethlehem, Penna. (May 20, 1984).

Shechtman, Stephen A. "With School Out, M-TV Has Even Less Competition," *The Sunday Globe Times*, Bethlehem, Penna. (July 15, 1984).

Singer, Wenda Goodhart; Shechtman, Stephen; and Singer, Mark. *Real Men Enjoy Their Kids! How to Spend Quality Time with the Children in Your Life.* Nashville: Abingdon Press, 1983.

Sugar, Max; Feinstein, Sherman C.; Looney, John G.; Schwartzberg, Allan Z.; and Sorosky, Arthur D., eds. *Adolescent Psychiatry: Developmental and Clinical*

Studies, Volume II. Chicago: University of Chicago Press, 1984.

Winship, E. C. *Reaching Your Teenager.* Boston: Houghton-Mifflin, 1983.

York, Phyllis; York, David; and Hochte, Ted. *Toughlove.* New York: Doubleday, 1982; Bantam Books, 1983.

RESOURCE AGENCIES

This list of national and local resources is not exhaustive. Human services in local communities can put the teen or parent in touch with resources that focus specifically upon personal or family problems. The authors suggest that family members use their local directories to locate essential human service organizations that can assist in alleviating serious emotional or relationship conflicts.

Local Services Available in Most Communities

Community/Neighborhood Centers
Catholic/Family Services
Community Mental Health Organizations
Family and Children Services
Jewish Family Services

National Services and Organizations

National Association for Children
with Learning Disabilities
4156 Library Road
Pittsburgh, PA 15234

RESOURCE AGENCIES

National Committee for Youth Services Prevention
230 Park Ave., Suite #835
New York, NY 10169

National Federation of Parents for Drug-Free Youth
P. O. Box 57217
Washington, DC 20037

National Institute on Drug Abuse
P.O. Box 2305
Rockville, MD 20852

National Peer Counseling Association Unit
of Educational Development
Bradley University
Peoria, IL 61625

Suicide Research Unit, NIMH
Rm. #10C26
5600 Fishers Lane
Rockville, MD 20857

Suicide Prevention Materials and Publications
Belle Willard Administration Center
10310 Layton Hall Drive
Fairfax, VA 22030

Suicide Hotline
(check local phone operators for the
number in your area)

National Runaway Switchboard
(nationwide toll-free service for crisis and referral)
(800) 621-4000

INDEX